Cymru

Cool Cymru Collection

Cool Cymru Collection

Photographer Terry Morris

GRAFFEG

Published by Graffeg
Hardback first published Autumn 2006
© Graffeg 2006
All images © Terry Morris 2006
ISBN-10: 1 905582 09 9

Graffeg, Radnor Court,
256 Cowbridge Road East
Cardiff CF5 1GZ Wales UK
Tel +44(0)29 2037 7312
sales@graffeg.com
www.graffeg.com

Designed and produced by
Peter Gill & Associates
sales@petergill.com
www.petergill.com

The Publisher acknowledges the financial
support of the Welsh Books Council.
www.gwales.com

Contents

Words **Pictures** Lighting

Andy Pearson Author

A journalist of 23 years, Andy took the Llanelli Star to several national awards as editor (2002-06). He has worked as a reporter for the Western Mail and as a sub-editor and features editor with the principality's biggest selling newspaper, the South Wales Evening Post. In the late 1990s he was a key driver in the launch and development of a series of South Wales nostalgia books that topped local sales charts. Andy was born in Brecon and raised in Yorkshire. He lives in Swansea with wife Claire, son Evan and daughter Millie. He rides around town on his beloved 125cc Vespa. His other passions include Huddersfield Town AFC, cricket, Timothy Taylor Landlord pale ale, ska, reggae, blues and jazz.

Terry Morris Photographer

Llanelli born and raised, Terry is a well respected and admired documentary photographer. Having spent many years working closely with the people of south Wales, he is now determined to revive the role of photography as an art and as an antidote to modern paparazzi culture. In doing so, he pledged to create Wales's first photographic hall of fame … and saw his project gather pace. Terry has gained broad life experience from his career with the British Armed Forces, his professional training in photography and visual art and then working for the press, which took him on assignments across the world. Terry lives in Llanelli with his partner Laura. He has a son, Conor, and a daughter, Sadie May.

Graham Harries Lighting Technician

Fed up with him constantly using their camera, Graham's parents bought him a Praktica MTL3 as a 13th birthday present in 1980. It was built like a brick. He has taken pictures ever since, with many other cameras. A member of Llanelli Photographic Society, Graham won the best monochrome print prize in 2002's Welsh Salon of Photography and has scooped numerous other awards. Graham has carried out freelance photography in the fields of press, PR and business. His passions include girlfriend Jayne Buckley, The Macallan single malt and rock music. He has a working relationship with Welsh band, Void. Born and raised in Llanelli, he has three children — Sam, 11, Beth, 10, and Meg, five.

U NTIL recently, Wales was the only country in Europe that did not have a dedicated children's hospital. Determined to change the situation and ensure that children in Wales should have access to the same care as other children throughout Europe, a group of dedicated people began a campaigning for a dedicated Children's Hospital for Wales.

Their tireless lobbying finally resulted in the National Assembly's approval for the project to go ahead with the money for the building to be raised through a charitable capital appeal.

The Noah's Ark Appeal was set up in May 2000 to raise the money needed to build the first phase of the first children's hospital for Wales. Many people, across Wales and beyond, were spurred into action to support the cause.
At the beginning of the Cool Cymru Collection process, Terry Morris approached the charity with an idea that would celebrate Welsh talent through an iconic photography collection and benefit the hospital financially. It proved to be a rewarding relationship.

The first phase of the Children's Hospital for Wales opened its doors to its first patients in February 2005. In stark contrast to the rundown paediatric wards, the Children's Hospital for Wales is bright, welcoming and child-friendly; it has been built with a child's perspective in mind. Floor patterns lead the way along each of the themed wards and nurses' stations are illuminated from below to guide children back to their rooms. Interactive art features on the walls of the hospital have the effect of making the hospital bright and cheerful and also a distraction from illness. Parents' needs are also catered for with pull-down beds for overnight stays and dedicated kitchen and rest areas.

Without the support and generosity of so many people, including star names, the Appeal couldn't have achieved what it has so far. However, it is vital that the Noah's Ark Appeal continues fundraising to support additional projects and facilities at the hospital to provide world-class care for generations of sick children in Wales.

To help please telephone 029 2033 5016 or visit www.noahs-ark-appeal.org

Introduction

HE may have been only a bit part player in a remarkable project, but Frank Corrente epitomised the spirit of the adventure.

Frank runs a car sales place in Los Angeles and knew nothing about Welsh photographer Terry Morris before Terry turned up on his forecourt with a Hollywood star.

Frank Corrente's Cadillac Corner is no ordinary motor business. It deals in classic American autos that have been either remarkably well kept by one careful owner or lovingly restored.

Gleaming chrome and polished sharkfins — those are the treasures he deals in. He offers everything from vintage 1930s convertibles to the Sedan DeVilles of the '90s plus Rolls-Royces and other luxurious and exotic models.

On the hot August morning when Terry arrived at his Sunset Boulevard business, Frank had given pride of place to a wow-factor old black Buick and a beautiful 1950 white convertible Cadillac.

Terry was accompanied by photographic muse Graham Harries and by Welsh actor Ioan Gruffudd, about to become the eighth entry in Terry's Cool Cymru Collection.

Frank — slicked back black hair, open-neck shirt, huge smile and big shades — has run his enterprise for more than four decades and, businessman that he remains, thought there might be a little money in the photo shoot. Once assured it was for a children's hospital charity, however, he agreed to Terry's request and dropped thoughts of payment.

The roof of his white Caddy was retracted and the windows eased down. Frank climbed into the car and wheeled it out slowly across the sidewalk. It was a majestic sight much appreciated by Terry, Graham and Ioan.

It was to be their photographic prop, where it stood, for 20 minutes.

"I'm glad I can help," said Frank. "It should make a good picture. People seem to like the look of these cars. A lot of celebrities come here to buy, and we've helped in a lot of movies.

"Photo shoots ain't my main thing but,

if it sounds like a worthwhile project, I'll do it.

"We've a great rapport with people from many countries; we've done business with the BBC and with Japan and Italy. I don't know about Wales, but I've done business with Australia — is that close?"

Terry got the picture he wanted and gave warm thanks to Frank.

The motor dealer's actions mirrored much of what had gone before in the photographer's 16-month quest to capture star names in original poses and to raise the profile of photography as an art, at the same time fundraising for the Children's Hospital for Wales.

It's hard to convince the managers and agents of some celebrities that a client's time would be well spent being photographed for free by a photographer not known to them — and for a project that's far from complete.

But Terry was determined to celebrate Welsh excellence, to recapture the spirit of thoughtful, artistic photography, and to explore the lasting, positive effects of the '90s Cool Cymru phenomenon. >

Frank — slicked back black hair, open-neck shirt, huge smile and big shades — has run his enterprise for more than four decades and, businessman that he remains, thought there might be a little money in the photo shoot. Once assured it was for a children's hospital charity, however, he agreed to Terry's request and dropped thoughts of payment.

Introduction

> From one tiny but ambitious thought, the process gathered an incredible head of steam resulting in trips to places as diverse as Cardiff and Chelsea, Llanelli and LA. Those pictured included film stars, music icons and sports heroes.

Most expressed a passing interest in photography as an art form. Most thought that bands such as the Stereophonics, the Manic Street Preachers and Catatonia had left a positive mark, as a Welsh nation so proud of its cultural roots looked to thrive in a new century with an expanding selection of stars.

The process was filmed for an ITV Wales documentary series and the collection secured exhibition slots around the country, including one at Cardiff's prestigious Wales Millennium Centre.

But it wouldn't have happened were it not for the welcome, cooperation, open-mindedness, humour and patience of people like Frank Corrente. Such qualities were amongst those shown by the big names targeted by Terry.

"Trends started to emerge right at the beginning, when I photographed Stuart Cable at a tattoo parlour in Llanelli," said Terry.

"The experience with Stuart was a kick up the backside to get me going. Success there drove me on to the next shoots. It gave me an impetus to get my next subject even though I knew it might take a lot of time, effort and breaking down of bureaucracy.

"So much depends on determination and a little bit of cheek. After all, if you don't ask, you don't get."

Charlotte Church was next, thanks to good work by strong contacts.

"Lyn Jones, the Noah's Ark chairman of trustees, fought our corner there," said Terry. "Lyn's friendly with Charlotte's mum, Maria. He spoke to her and, out of the blue one day, she phoned me.

"I explained what I was doing and she said it sounded great. She gave me Charlotte's mobile number and told me to give her a ring.

"I had a cuppa and a fag before I called, to pluck up courage. After I'd explained things to Charlotte she said, 'That sounds grand — I'll meet you in Llanelli'."

The singer showed exceptional patience during her photo shoot as she stood behind a sheet of cold water, being inadvertently splashed, for two hours.

"She was great," said Terry. "She was a real professional who showed an incredible amount of spirit."

Gavin Henson exhibited similar qualities when he was asked to squeeze his bulky, rugby player's frame into a small cage. Terry said, "The process took around three hours and he proved to be a thoroughly decent guy."

The trend continued as staff and stars at St David's Hall in Cardiff and at Manchester United offered effort and hospitality.

In the case of Rhys Ifans, a strong element of family networking proved the key. Terry said, "Apparently his mother had urged him to do the shoot because she'd been talking to a family friend — Catrin Mears — who was working for PR company Merlin who were with me on the project.

"He made a joke of it on the day, along the lines of, 'If you want to get somebody in Wales to do something, ask their mother'."

There were plenty of laughs with Dame Shirley Bassey too.

In London, as she posed behind a scattering of diamonds worth more than £1million and loaned by New Bond Street business Asprey, Terry cheekily winked at her and said, "I'm taking some of those diamonds home."

She replied, "You'll be lucky, darling. I did some filming for the BBC some years ago. Diamonds were supplied, but they were weighed before the shoot ... and after."

Another key constant was Graham Harries, a strong photographer in his own right, who supplied much technical support, artistic inspiration and all-areas back-up from day one.

"He was a great help and top class company," said Terry. "We had a lot of fun along the way, like when he thought he'd lost his passport at Los Angeles International Airport and when a TV camera he was using broke down in the same city, resulting in a mad 90-minute scramble to hire one.

"Also, there must still be dozens of people in Hollywood still thinking what on earth a fella was doing, leaning out of a Buick and shouting, 'S'mae, But!'

"Earlier, in Llanelli, Graham' took great delight in splashing water at Charlotte Church — there aren't many fellas who can say they've done that!

"He's also the one who posed for test shots before we did the real shoot. It was hilarious watching this Llanelli dad pretending to be Charlotte Church or Dame Shirley Bassey.

"He was even good value when the laugh was on him. He ordered a cappuccino at an Italian restaurant in Battersea and, as this big mug was being carried over, the waited tripped and sent the contents flying towards Graham's lap. He saw the funny side when he realised it had been a comic trip and the 'cappuccino' was just a lump of painted foam."

Another impression that will live long in Terry's memory is that of how Wales's celebrities enjoy keeping their feet on the ground.

He said, "They were all brilliant to work with. None gave me grief and all gave their time, warmth, cooperation, open-mindedness and patience. I couldn't have asked for any more."

"I'm delighted it all came together so well, despite all the obstacles. I've learnt a lot, so perhaps now I'll start on halls of fame for Ireland, Scotland and England ... "

To all you managers, agents, stars and Frank Correntes out there: Watch out! ■

Stuart

Cable

Stuart Cable Setting the scene

Monday, May 23, 2005

HEADTEACHER Leighton Rees is dressed like a hippy. His wig is blond and black, his headband red. Leighton's pupils — aged from three to 11 — are loving it. Some of them are dressed in gear reflecting the trends of Britain's Elizabethan and Georgian times.

They're gathered under a bright spring sky at the top of a steep hillside rising out of one of Wales's great industrial townscapes — terraced, backstreet Llanelli.

Forget algebra and English grammar for a short while, they've been told, enjoy your through-the-ages day.

Photographer Terry Morris is there to capture some of the action as a freelance commission for local paper the Llanelli Star. In his time at the paper he's done many similar jobs. Bigyn Community Primary School usually brings a smile to his face.

"The head's a really nice guy," says Terry. "He thinks the world of the kids, and it shows on a day like this. They're lapping it up because they've been allowed to come dressed as they like — they've picked a period and their mums have dressed them up.

"There are some fantastic costumes. Some kids look like they've come off a TV set. I'll have some great pictures because it's such a fun event.

"I must admit, though, that I didn't spot the head for a while. With his hippy clothes, his wig and headband, I didn't recognise him. I've taken one un-posed picture of him and he's begged me not to use it — but it wouldn't surprise me if someone back at the office was cheeky enough to put it in the paper. It'd all be in fun, of course, and I know Leighton would take it the right way."

The school's position on top of Bigyn Hill allows wonderful views as far as the Black Mountains to the north, Tenby and Caldey Island to the west and Gower to the east. Terry has a last look around before descending to the Star's town centre office.

Bigyn may have a rich schooling history stretching back to the 1870s, but it's the immediate future that Terry is most concerned with — this week's paper.

"I'm also thinking about lunch," he smiles. "The Savoy chippy's opposite the Star — and me and my partner Laura fancy a sit-down there."

His partner, Laura Grime, is the Star's chief reporter and she's on newsdesk duty when he returns. She's on the phone and is delighted to see him.

"It's Rod the tattooist," Laura reveals over a muffled mouthpiece. "He's got Cable at his place, Stuart Cable. Can you get down there?"

Rod Morris is a former school pal of Terry who knows an opportunity for publicity when he sees it. He has called the Star, knowing that any small town newspaper would be interested in the visit of a founding member of one of Wales's top rock bands.

Stuart's time with the Stereophonics had ended in 2003 after 18 hit singles and four top-selling albums, but he still has rock star news value. Terry's eyes light up.

Terry takes the phone from Laura. "Rod, I'll be over in five minutes."

Stuart doesn't know it yet, but he's one of the Welsh celebrities Terry plans to photograph as part of a new project.

"It's Rod the tattooist," Laura reveals over a muffled mouthpiece. "He's got Cable at his place, Stuart Cable. Can you get down there?"

"The thing's very much in its early days at the moment," says Terry. "I've emailed some people but haven't had any response yet. If I'm careful in presenting the whole idea to Stuart perhaps he'll become my first subject — that'd give me a real nudge to go on and do more."

Fridays are busy in Llanelli and traffic is brisk as Terry sets off on foot via Cowell Street and Murray Street. Station Road is a four-minute walk. It can become five with a heavy camera bag.

The tattoo parlour is one of those places that, viewed from the outside, could be any number of businesses. A glance down Station Road doesn't reveal a tattoo parlour, just a number of places that could be taxi offices or barber shops.

"I've not met Stuart and I've not been inside this parlour," admits Terry. "I don't know what to expect from this job — but working as a press photographer teaches you to think on your feet."

On arrival at the parlour the photographer's mind races back to Bigyn's fancy dress scholars.

"Rock'n'roll," purrs Terry. "I expected Cable in jeans and T-shirt but he's here in a cowboy hat, Cuban heels, vest and ripped jeans. He's the epitome of rock'n'roll — this is going to be great." ▪

Stuart Cable

Hotrod'z tattoo parlour, Llanelli
Monday, May 23, 2005

Stuart Cable The thought process

Monday, May 23, 2005

A GANGSTER film wouldn't be complete without one. You've seen rugged leading men being pampered in one and motormouth barbers chewing cigars over one. You've seen bit part characters have their throats slit in one.

America's evocative barber shop chairs have seen more movie action than some Hollywood greats and more horror than some of Tinseltown's most grizzly X-rated flicks.

And Terry Morris adores them.

The hushed hydraulics, lush leather upholstery and sparkling chrome fittings make for a design classic. They recline, they swivel, they have padded footplates. Control of their levers and sliders would challenge some of the brightest crane operators.

"I love all that stuff," says the photographer as he peers inside one of two booths at Hotrod'z tattoo parlour in Llanelli's Station Road.

"The old American diner bar stools that look like they've really been engineered, and the big, solid barber chairs with all their chrome — fantastic.

"A lot of the stuff you see in furniture shops today looks too plastic for me — it doesn't look as if it's made to last.

"The old chairs like you see in Rod Morris's tattoo place are much more to my liking. The great '50s styling makes them really photogenic."

Terry's eye has been caught by one of the tattoo parlour's barber shop chairs. Musician and broadcaster Stuart Cable is about to sink into one of them as his left arm is decorated with another piece of inky art.

"This picture could be nothing without that chair," says Terry. "That piece of furniture will help make it."

That, as well as Stuart's dress code, of course, which contrasts starkly with a Station Road so working class that it still has £6-a-cut barber shops, a pub called the Rolling Mill and takeaways that feed thousands every week.

Stuart is sporting a Stetson-shaped straw hat, a white vest, ripped jeans and a pair of much-loved cowboy boots. If ever a photographer need supply no props for a picture, this is it.

Rod and Stuart think the camera man is at the parlour simply for a photo that will make the pages of this week's Llanelli Star — but the visitor has a second motive. He wants to take this opportunity to kick-start his Wales hall of fame project.

Over a cup of tea, and amongst animated talk of Welsh rugby, Terry sells the project's concept to the drummer. He explains to Stuart that he'd love a shot of him in the chair, Rod working on his arm.

"Yeah, I'll be part of that — no worries," says Stuart. "Just do what you have to."

Terry finds that the available light in the salon — provided by large street-view windows — and the stillness of his seated subject, means all he has to worry about is angle and framing.

A worm's eye view is chosen, so that a blank wall is the background rather than some of Rod's artwork, hundreds of examples of which are pinned on some areas of wall. Impressive though they are, the tattoos would complicate the final image. >

Terry's eye has been caught by one of the tattoo parlour's barber shop chairs. Musician and broadcaster Stuart Cable is about to sink into one of them as his left arm is decorated with another piece of inky art.

"The picture was a spur of the moment thing — it wasn't as if I had a week to think about it, to consider what I was going to do."

> Framing is achieved with part of the chair on one side and part of Rod's face on the other.

With the image in the can, Terry is delighted. He says: "The picture was a spur of the moment thing — it wasn't as if I had a week to think about it, to consider what I was going to do.

"There was no extended thought process — only when I saw Stuart and what he was wearing did the cogs start turning. When I saw the chair I knew the setting was perfect. I didn't have to do anything. It could've been a hopeless shot had the parlour only had a little plastic chair and had Stuart been dressed in different clothes, with no hat.

"I'm so excited about this picture because I've thought about this project for a long time and now, suddenly, I've taken the first picture. This is the start of the project — now I've really got to make it work." ▪

Stuart Cable The interview

Monday, May 23, 2005

SITTING back in a comfy chair with a good pal working his artistic magic on a treasured new creation is one idea of bliss for Stuart Cable.

And the former Stereophonics drummer insists that all these boxes are ticked for him in Llanelli's Hotrod'z tattoo parlour.

The chair is an old-style barbershop special, the friend is Rod Morris and the fresh work is a vision in flowers and hearts at the top of Stuart's left arm.

The musician's muscular drumming once gave his arms tough regular workouts in the recording studio and, more graphically, on stage — but now they're at ease with Rod being the one taking the strain.

"I find having a tattoo really relaxing," smiles Stuart. "It's addictive because once you've had one piece done there's an imbalance — you stand in front of the mirror and realise that you need to get a piece done on the other side of your body.

"It's great to see a beautiful piece of work being created. In my case, I look at what Rod is doing and start thinking just what else he could achieve if I asked.

"Maybe I'll end up asking him to tattoo me in lots of other places, other than my arms."

Stuart began developing a passion for tattoos during his time with the band. He saw it as a contrast to the intensity of the rock'n'roll lifestyle.

He says, "Playing with the Stereophonics was hectic. There were days of 12 to 15 hours, with everything from promo shoots to gigs. We often lived life off a sheet of paper.

"When I came home I did my best to have as much fun as possible. I bought myself a couple of motorbikes, took up golf and started thinking about having tattoos."

He had wanted some tattoo work done but didn't know where to go for the best results. A cameraman friend who worked on his small screen show Cable TV, and who lived in the Llanelli village of Hendy, recommended Rod.

Stuart says, "Me and Rod hit it off straight away, as friends. Early on I took him some magazine pictures and designs I liked. Rod said that'd be a good starting point for deciding what I wanted on my arm."

Looking back on his Stereophonics days, Stuart now puts forward a considered view on the Cool Cymru tag applied to the 1990s interest centred on key Welsh pop culture icons of the time.

He says, "Cool Cymru was a name, probably invented by a journalist from London, who needed to come up with a label. There seems to be a need for the papers in London to put everything in a category.

"Actually, the bands at the centre of Cool Cymru — ourselves, Catatonia, the Manic Street Preachers and the Super Furry Animals — were all very different. It was a coincidence that we were all popular at the same time.

"There was one point, I seem to remember, when Welsh bands held the top three places in the UK's album charts — and I'm sure success like that inspired some kids to take up the guitar, drums or bass and to form their own bands.

"I wouldn't really have called it Cool Cymru because there was never a scene as such, like there was in Seattle. We weren't the same as each other, we were totally different — and that was a good thing.

"In any case, I think it's always been cool to be Welsh," says Stuart. "You didn't need a bunch of bands to make being Welsh cool. Jobs are harder to come by these days, with the decline of the coal industry and so on, but I've never met anyone who's not proud to be Welsh.

"We've got a brilliant capital, in Cardiff — it's got great facilities like the Millennium Stadium and the Bay, but we've also got loads of places that retain a real traditional community spirit, like Aberdare and Llanelli.

"In so many places in Wales you still know your next door neighbour and can still get a local builder and plumber to do some work for you. Whatever job you want done you can just pop down the local pub. To a large extent, I don't think even the capital, with all its developments, has lost that.

"Wales has always been a diverse and robust set of communities and there are still a lot of values and tradition. I've lived here all my life and have never stopped loving it."

Hall of Fame Fact File

- Stuart Cable was born in 1970.

- With Cwmaman school pals Kelly Jones and Richard Jones, he formed the Stereophonics in 1992 and they went on to become one of Britain's biggest bands.

- In March 2002 Stuart fronted a campaign, Bllcks, to raise awareness of testicular cancer. It was hosted by BBC Wales and supported by the Welsh Assembly Government.

- Cable TV and radio's Cable Rock are among the broadcast shows Stuart has presented.

Charlotte

Church

Charlotte Church Setting the scene

Wednesday, December 14, 2005

A SHEET of cold water is tumbling from a grey metal tank 12 feet off the ground in a huge room. It falls with a constant crash into another tank, this one deeper and made of black plastic.

At the sides of the tanks are two towers of building site scaffolding. A bridging structure between them holds the upper tank.

The whole thing is ugly, it's industrial and its purpose seems indistinct.

Yet this is the sight that's about to greet one of Wales's most high-profile women.

Just what Charlotte Church is going to make of the rig for her latest photo shoot is anyone's guess. How it relates to her career in song and celebrity is also unclear.

Photographer Terry Morris is increasingly anxious as the minutes pass because he has never met Charlotte — and he can't predict her reaction to the stark, unfamiliar scene that will greet her when she arrives at this former Tesco supermarket that now houses TV and new media company, Tinopolis, in Llanelli.

There are other reasons to be wary too.

"It's taken a week to get this rig right," says Terry. "At times it's been a nightmare — so much thought, science, design and care has gone in to it."

He wants Charlotte to be photographed while peeping through an inverted v-shape slash in a curtain of falling water.

The first problem has been creating the curtain.

This is considerably tougher than it sounds — try it at home in the bath with a family-sized ice cream tub.

The second problem has been creating the v-shape. Sorry, you won't be able to try this at home because your water curtain efforts will have failed.

To tackle the water challenge, Terry has called in Llanelli electrical engineer John Treharne, a pal from days when they worked together around Europe, constructing hi-tech installations for entertainment venues.

On one trip to Germany, a shopping centre had been having a large mock waterfall feature built. John had taken a close interest in its mechanics.

"It's that particular experience he's brought to this," says Terry. "He's a switched-on cookie and, even though water can be difficult to control, he's done the business for me.

"John designed the rig and I helped him put it up.

"It has been tricky, though. For two days the thing didn't work — the water wouldn't behave and we still didn't have it right a day or two ago. But John made the adjustments and has created just what I wanted."

The v-shape has been a challenge for Terry and his photographic lighting man Graham Harries.

They have experimented for several hours behind the waterfall, using Graham's fingers to make the point of the V in the water.

"It took us days to suss out," says Terry. "We took shot after shot because the water wouldn't do just as we wanted. But we got there in the end. Now we know exactly what to tell Charlotte.

Terry Morris is increasingly anxious as the minutes pass because he has never met Charlotte — and he can't predict her reaction to the stark, unfamiliar scene that will greet her when she arrives at this former Tesco supermarket.

"However, the shoot won't be easy because it all hinges on tiny changes in the angle of fingers, and the precision with which they're held in place, just above the right brow."

There's one other problem today. Around 50 miles away in Cardiff, Charlotte's moving home. ▪

Charlotte Church

Tinopolis studios, Llanelli
Wednesday, December 14, 2005

Charlotte Church The thought process

Wednesday, December 14, 2005

HIS subject may be only 19 years old — but trying to think up an original photograph of her proved difficult for Terry Morris.

He flicked through countless magazines, newspapers and web pages to understand what had been done before.

CD covers, video grabs, film stills and paparazzi snaps were studied as he hunted for inspiration on a unique view of Charlotte Church.

"I've seen semi-nudes, a geisha girl look, the coy school girl images and the sophisticated pop queen promotional shots," says Terry.

He researched the subject with partner Laura Grime. It was over a simple cup of tea, however, that something finally clicked. For no particular reason the couple got onto the subject of water.

Laura mentioned a TV ad that featured a crashing tropical waterfall.

"It'd be nice to have a waterfall crashing down on Charlotte," Terry told Laura.

"But I can tell you're thinking of something different."

She said, "Wouldn't it be good to picture Charlotte behind the water, looking out?"

The idea was born.

And that's still the idea as Charlotte leaves behind a day of moving house in Cardiff to take the M4 west to Llanelli's town centre Tinopolis studios.

She arrives mid-morning, ahead of time and clutching a mug of tea as she strolls into the studio, set aside for this photo shoot.

Charlotte is greeted by Terry, his lighting man Graham Harries, a Tinopolis TV film crew and a wide, 12ft tall structure of steel and plastic, the like of which she's never seen.

Central to the structure is a metre-wide sheet of cold water.

Charlotte takes the unfamiliarity in her stride and chooses a delicate, full-length red dress from a selection hand-picked by Terry. As her hair and make-up are being attended to, she chats

animatedly about the rigours of moving house and the excitement of not knowing what boyfriend Gavin Henson has bought for her imminent birthday.

The singer takes up an uncomfortable position behind the waterfall and tentatively places two fingers of her right hand in front of her forehead and into the water.

Getting the desired effect is tricky, one problem being that the noise of the water means Terry's instructions to Charlotte — around 10ft away — must be conveyed through Graham who sits to one side of the waterfall.

There's also a problem with water splashing back into Charlotte's eyes. Hundreds of shots are taken with Terry's digital Nikon, and it is only after two hours of trial and error that there's success.

He says, "I take my hat off to Charlotte. She's been here three hours and has had her fingers in cold water for half that time — her fingers are red raw now.

"We've had cups of tea and ceramic heaters to warm her up a bit, but it was a long time for her to stand there, >

Charlotte is greeted by Terry, his lighting man Graham Harries, a Tinopolis TV film crew and a wide, 12ft tall structure of steel and plastic, the like of which she's never seen. Central to the structure is a metre-wide sheet of cold water.

> getting ever more wet as time went on.

"But she has been so professional. I think everyone's been impressed by her attitude.

"Amazingly, at one point, she even asked if water droplets on her face looked good and was happy for Graham to flick some more at her.

"That's something he'll be telling the grandkids in a few years — 'I flicked water at a superstar singer's face'." ∎

"Amazingly, at one point, she even asked if water droplets on her face looked good and was happy for Graham to flick some more at her."

Terry Morris wanted Charlotte Church to be photographed while peeping through an inverted v-shape slash in a curtain of falling water. The first problem was creating the curtain. This was considerably tougher than it sounds.

Hall of Fame Fact File

- Charlotte was born in 1986.

- Her debut album was released in 1998. Voice of an Angel sold more than 600,000 copies in the UK as Charlotte became the youngest artist to top the classical chart.

- Global success led to the publication of an autobiography at the age of 16.

- Summer 2005 saw the release of her first pop single, Crazy Chick.

Gavin

Henson

Gavin Henson Setting the scene

Friday, February 10, 2006

A YEAR and five days ago a young man produced a wonderful moment of skill that immediately entered the consciousness of a game already chock-a-block with great memories.

The game was Welsh rugby, the man Gavin Henson, the treasure an angled penalty kick of around 40 metres which sealed his nation's first win over England — the world champions — in six years.

The kick had been taken in the dying stages of a hard-fought match in front of almost 74,200 fans at Cardiff's Millennium Stadium. Millions had watched on TV.

Most observers would have failed to function normally under such pressure, but this 23-year-old, in red shirt, white shorts, red socks and silver-coloured boots, had kept his cool, focussed brilliantly and won the game.

An indication of how much victory, and this single kick, meant to his countrymen came from Wales skipper Gareth Thomas. He told journalists: "I feel like I could fly right now."

Gavin's magic moment brought praise from around the rugby-playing world. Planet-Rugby.com stated: "Henson was the undisputed star of the show."

A writer for respected Scottish newspaper The Scotsman reported: "Rugby players do not come more confident or courageous than Gavin Henson."

Former England and British Lions player Jeremy Guscott was reported by BBC Online to have said of Gavin: "It's difficult to get across how much class he has - he's majestic."

Wales went on to win their four subsequent games in that RBS Six Nations tournament to record a grand slam, a 100% winning record.
It was an emotional time for a country that uses its rugby as a standard bearer for national pride and identity.

Yet this depth of feeling also has its downsides. It is one reason that, as Gavin prepares for today's photo shoot with Terry Morris, his status as a hero is being questioned.

A summer tour of New Zealand with the British Lions didn't go to plan, with key games being lost and with Gavin playing a limited role. The first half of the 2005-06 season saw him injured and banned.

By today he has played only three competitive games in six months.

An autobiography that did excellent business at Christmas brought trouble for Gavin on the rugby circuit. Some team-mates didn't like what he had written about them.

Moreover, many rugby supporters now dislike the fact that Welsh TV, radio and newspapers — and some sections of the wider British media — seem obsessed by Gavin's flourishing relationship with singer Charlotte Church.

Terry is concerned that today's subject will have taken such a hard mental hit from his roller coaster ride that the shoot could be difficult.

The photographer says: "From what I've seen on TV he's a decent guy and I suspect that, beneath the swagger on the rugby pitch, he's a little shy.

"I suspect the sudden way he's been thrust into the media spotlight has come as a shock to him. >

The game was Welsh rugby, the man Gavin Henson, the treasure an angled penalty kick of around 40 metres which sealed his nation's first win over England — the world champions — in six years.

> He's probably a genuine, quiet guy.

"My guess, also, is that he needs to be applauded when he's done something good — I think that he needs appreciation so he knows he's on the right track.

"When he's going through a good patch, when he's playing well, he's upbeat and confident — but when he's going through a bad patch, I suspect, he kind of goes into his shell.

"That's the only thing that concerns me today — the fact that he's been going through a bad patch for eight months.

"I bet he's taken a real knock on the book controversy and I don't plan to discuss anything about the past few months — or even about rugby. I think there are too many negatives bound up in all that and I think the best photo with Gavin will come when the circumstances are as positive as possible."

With that Terry looks hopefully at the place where he'd like the rugby player to be photographed. It's a cage, similar to those that house chickens at livestock marts. It measures around three feet long by two and a half feet deep. It's about two feet wide. ▪

Terry looks hopefully at the place where he'd like the rugby player to be photographed. It's a cage, similar to those that house chickens at livestock marts.

Gavin Henson

Tinopolis studios, Llanelli
Friday, February 10, 2006

Gavin Henson **The thought process**

Friday, February 10, 2006

LANELLI'S former town centre Tesco is now a roomy base for TV and new media firm Tinopolis. Terry Morris is due to spend a few hours there today, photographing Gavin Henson.

The photographer was there yesterday with right-hand man Graham Harries, discussing the shoot. At one point, they entered a long corridor punctuated by TV props and pieces of old show sets. As their gazes wandered, both fixed upon a silver-coloured steel cuboid cage. Terry shared his thoughts.

"I wonder if you could get an adult in that," he said to his pal, who is to act as a surrogate celebrity when test shots are being taken for the Gavin shoot. Graham's brow wrinkled and his eyes widened.

"If you think you're getting me in there you can take a hike," he grimaced. "It's small, it doesn't look comfortable and I don't think anyone — let alone Gavin Henson — would take kindly to being asked to suffer like that."

A few minutes later, however, Graham was in the cage. He looked trapped and uncomfortable, like a chimp in a budgie cage.

Terry liked the look. He thought Gavin inside the cage would help create a memorable image. Graham was let out for the night.

As Friday morning develops, Gavin, having driven west from Cardiff, parks at Llanelli's out-of-town McDonald's and phones Terry. Graham goes to meet the guest and to guide him to the studio.

Terry, meanwhile, puts the finishing touches to his props — and reveals that he plans to spend the early part of the photo shoot gaining Gavin's confidence. He wants to understand how the guest's mind is working.

Terry says, "Gavin's had a few rough months and I don't want to push my luck. Before I mention the cage idea I'll ask him to lean between a couple of Trilites, trusses of narrow tubular poles joined together by criss-cross aluminium rods. They're used in stage designs, for TV show sets and at events that need smart-looking presentations.

"They'll signify a modern approximation of the traditional rugby posts, and I think they'll be something that Gavin won't feel intimidated by. Once we've

got some decent pictures in the can with the Trilites I'll mention the cage.

"It's small, cramped and was once used by a Tinopolis TV show that featured some caged birds."

Gavin arrives. He's quiet but friendly and is quickly into the photo shoot. He poses between the posts in his black suit and white shirt. During a break in shooting he studies Terry's pictures on Graham's laptop and likes what he sees. But it's time to mention the cage. Terry says, "See that? I'd love to try something with the cage."

Gavin chuckles and says, "Don't think I haven't seen it — and, yes, I was wondering what it'd be for."

Terry says, "I don't want to force you to do anything — but I think the cage would give a nice shape to the picture. It must have been great, touring with the British Lions last summer — and now I'd like to photograph a caged Lion."

Gavin's eyes light up. He likes the idea. The shoot can continue.

The rugby player, barefooted but in his elegant black suit, kneels on the floor and crawls backwards into the cage. It's a squeeze and Gavin laughs to himself as if to ask: "What on earth am I getting myself into?"

Graham helps him in and forces the flap closed, keeping his feet tightly on it in order to push down the clips.

The cage is leaning heavily and looks as if it could tip over, but Gavin centres his gravity and awaits Terry's instructions.

Graham directs a light from the side, adjusting its position to create lines of light and shadow across Gavin's semi-illuminated face.

The rugby star has his hands fully inside the cage — but as he makes a slight adjustment some fingers on the right hand poke out of the cage.

"Hang on," says Terry, "the hand looks nice out of the top."

It doesn't take long before the photographer has the photo he wants.

"I like these shots," he says. "This picture's in the bag — and it's great that you've been so patient."

The Lion is invited out of the cage. He unfurls himself and peeks at the latest photos on Graham's laptop.

He says, "Great — whichever one of those you pick should be a great picture."

Although the shoot appears to be over Gavin has no qualms about experimenting further, even when Terry asks him to strip to his boxer shorts to see how a caged Lion would appear without the protection of an Armani suit.

But the results don't impress Terry. One of the shots with the suit will be his final choice. ▪

Hall of Fame
Fact File

- Gavin was born in 1982.

- He was educated at Brynteg Comprehensive School, Bridgend.

- On the subject of Henson's place in rugby, Jon Henderson wrote in national Sunday newspaper The Observer, "He has almost single-handedly ushered the Welsh game out of the age of scrubbed-scalp, gap-toothed boyos into the new one of Cool Cymru." (Guardian Newspapers Limited 2005)

- Hellomagazine.com lists Henson among three "Celtic hunks" alongside actors Ioan Gruffudd and Christian Bale.

Gavin Henson leant between a couple of Trilites, trusses of narrow tubular poles joined together by criss-cross aluminium rods. Terry Morris said they signifed a modern approximation of traditional rugby posts.

Terry says, "See that? I'd love to
try something with the cage."
Gavin chuckles and says,
"Don't think I haven't seen it — and,
yes, I was wondering what it'd be for."

Bryn

Terfel

Bryn Terfel Setting the scene

Saturday, April 22, 2006

THE stage door of St David's Hall isn't a place the poets go to embrace the changing of the seasons.

It's as distant from nature's most remarkable phenomena as you get.

A dowdy concrete ramp, a few scuffed yards of tubular steel railing and a clanking roller-shutter door do not together make for a traditional focus of verse.

It's more Kwik Save loading bay than meandering Cambrian Mountains riverbank. It's not a place for quiet contemplation on how spring is sprung.

Yet Terry Morris is fired up as Cardiff's temperatures soar.

"Summer's here," he says as he and lighting man Graham Harries lug a dozen black items of photographic baggage out of Morris's Land Rover Freelander and up the ramp. "Summer starts today and there'll be no looking back.

"It's been a long winter but summer's going to be longer still."

Were he to refer to it, his desk diary would tell him that the official start of summer — the solstice — is two months away. But nobody is about to deny this lover of the photographic art a hint of dreamer's optimism.

After all, the capital's skies are a hazy grey-blue and city centre shoppers are stripped down to their favourite T-shirts.

Moreover, we're soon to be in the company of an orchestra that symbolises the way that, as the seasons move on, stars of the performing arts also come and go.

Some young members of Sinfonia Cymru will remain committed to being solid team players, out of the individual spotlight. Others have what it takes to be big name musicians of the future.

As they rehearse in the main auditorium of St David's Hall, it's clear that there's much genuine talent on show.

Their programme tonight is due to feature Beethoven's challenging Piano Concerto No 5.

The event has been promoted as the Sinfonia's 10th anniversary concert —

and the musicians are delighted to be welcoming four choirs, a remarkable young Welsh pianist and four distinguished soloists.

The ivories man is Llyr Williams, a popular collaborator with the Sinfonia and the recipient of much acclaim. He is just 30.

The soloists include hard-working County Durham soprano Claire Rutter; well travelled Welsh mezzo soprano Leah-Marian Jones; award-winning young American tenor Gregory Turay; and the focus of Terry's attentions, North Wales bass baritone Bryn Terfel.

As Terry's bags add to the backstage clutter of the Sinfonia's cello cases, Bryn is at the other end of a windowless breeze block corridor. He's relaxing in a small changing room.

He rehearsed in the early afternoon and is now considering how to relax in the run-up to the concert.

There's an eagerly awaited Chelsea v Liverpool FA Cup semi-final being shown on TV in some Cardiff pubs — and there's the Terry Morris photo shoot being set up on stage as Sinfonia members >

As Terry's bags add to the backstage clutter of the Sinfonia's cello cases, Bryn is at the other end of a windowless breeze block corridor. He's relaxing in a small changing room.

> depart for a couple of hours R&R before the expectations of an anticipated full house are honoured.

On this pale wooden stage, the elegant kettle drums, music stands and jet black Steinway grand provide a balletic contrast to the heavy metal roadie functionality of the stage door.

It is this reverent auditorium where the fourth hall of fame photo is to be created. ▥

On this pale wooden stage, the elegant kettle drums, music stands and jet black Steinway grand provide a balletic contrast to the heavy metal roadie functionality of the stage door.

52

Bryn Terfel The thought process

Saturday, April 22, 2006

RAMROD straight, poised, prepared, and in command of his skills, his art and his audience.

As Bryn Terfel is pictured preparing to fulfil his latest starring role, he is the manifestation of sure-footed professionalism.

He knows where he's from, he has a good idea of where he's going and he's in full control of this performance.

But what about the times when he's not at his most public? What about the hours and minutes before a big show? What's the man like then, before the music-loving public have hopped in their cars and taxis to head off for the concert hall?

That's the image Terry Morris wants to capture as his photographic rig is assembled on stage in the main auditorium of St David's Hall, Cardiff.

"Most people will see Bryn as a man in a dinner suit, a man gazing assuredly out into an audience, with the full might of an orchestra behind him," says Terry.

"My portrayal of him has to be different — one that will surprise his fans. I hope he's in jeans, a T-shirt and a scruffy pair of boots.

"I'd like to see him with a chewed polystyrene cup in his hand, studying a dog-eared newspaper — an image as far removed from opera as there is."

However, in case the casual approach of Bryn in his civvies doesn't work, Terry has also asked that the singer can perform a quick change into a dinner suit.

At 5.15pm, leaving his dressing room for the stage, Bryn is in casual gear — a blue short-sleeved check shirt, dark jeans and a much-loved pair of robust get-about shoes.

It's just what Terry wants, and he asks Bryn to sit on a chair in the middle of equipment set up for the night's Sinfonia Cymru concert. To accentuate the relaxed feel, both feet are planted on another chair, the flat, scuffed faces of the shoes' soles peering straight into the lens.

The newspaper thought has given way to Bryn holding Sinfonia sheet music due to the attractive nature of such documents and because they provide a direct link with the night's performance.

However, the images taken on stage aren't to Terry's liking. The tones of the leisure clothes seem at odds with an attractive image. The black tie effect will work better.

Bryn disappears for his change. He's not long in returning — and Terry's eyes light up.

"He shines in the tux," says the photographer. "He seems equally relaxed in this gear as he did in the other stuff."

The singer is back on the chair, with his music sheets, happily peering into the distance, appearing pensive in some frames, smiling warmly in others.

"Bryn's such a warm fella," says Terry, "that I've got to capture that smile. That's Bryn Terfel — warm, happy and at ease with his role in life.

"I met him a few months ago when the Llanelli Star asked me to photograph him at a book signing in the town's Asda. On that occasion I put to him the possibility of appearing in the hall >

"Bryn's such a warm fella," says Terry, "that I've got to capture that smile. That's Bryn Terfel — warm, happy and at ease with his role in life."

> of fame and he was lovely, approachable and thoughtful. That's just how he's being today."

In an effort to work in a further element of surprise, the singer is asked to strike a similar pose in an auditorium seat, three or four rows from the front. It's where his audience would least expect to bump into him.

But it's the previous shot that Terry favours. The only question is: "Should I go for the long shot, using the soles of the shoes as a starting point for the viewers and drawing them up to the face through a hint of trouser and jacket — or should I simply let the face and the music say it all?"

That's a thought to consider as the weeks race towards the hall of fame's exhibition launch. ■

Terry Morris takes a worm's eye view of his subject.

"I met him a few months ago when the Llanelli Star asked me to photograph him at a book signing in the town's Asda. On that occasion I put to him the possibility of appearing in the hall of fame and he was lovely, approachable and thoughtful. That's just how he's being today."

Bryn Terfel The thought process

The St David's Hall side stalls.

In civvies – a casual look between rehearsal and performance.

Bryn Terfel The thought process

Things are looking up in the St David's Hall auditorium.

Bryn Terfel shone in his dinner suit, according to Terry Morris – even when he was having his hair groomed for the St David's Hall photo shoot.

Bryn Terfel The thought process

Bryn Terfel has a laugh during his photo shoot.

A seat on centre stage.

Bryn Terfel The interview

Saturday, April 22, 2006

MUCH of Bryn Terfel's professional life happens in vibrant colour. Heading up Tosca at Covent Garden's ravishing Royal Opera House or fronting his own concerts in Kiev and Moscow, the singer is immersed in the spectacular.

The tone of his surroundings can sometimes match that of his wonderful bass baritone.

The setting for his annual open air summer festival — amongst the muscular hills of Faenol — is a breathtaking landscape of rich Welsh green. Surely such colour must influence the man.

Yet some of Bryn's treasured artefacts at home are in stark contrast to this.

His love of photography harks back to the world's ebbing and flowing passion for stylish, black and white portraiture.

Sitting in his understated, monotone backstage room at St David's Hall, Cardiff, Bryn reveals that Terry Morris's desire to recapture some of David Bailey's '60s spirit sits comfortably with him.

"I collect black and white photographs," he says. "The prints I've got are mainly of people I'm interested in.

"The images I've got hanging around the house represent a diverse set of subjects. They range from Italian tenor Franco Corelli to Laurel and Hardy.

"I'm a huge fan of the fact that there are people who take these photos and that the images are there to be collected by people who're interested in them."

Among photographers to have won his admiration are Snowden and Lichfield.

"I was very happy to have a picture taken in Cardiff by Lichfield," he says.

"It all looked so easy when he did it, yet so much hard work and dedication must go in to mastering such a form.

"I'm sure that must be a common factor between those who make it to the top in photography and those who do the same in classical music. It's through knowing their art that they succeed in it."

In fast-moving times of digital video clips being enjoyed almost instantly on the home PC, Bryn says that stills photography retains its relevance as a documentary form.

"It's difficult to pick one defining image I've seen," he says. "There are so many of them. But just look at those harrowing images from 9/11."

Some photography, he finds less compulsive.

He says, "It's wonderful that there are celebrities in Wales, although some of them, like Gavin Henson and Charlotte Church, seem to be hounded by the paparazzi. I'd absolutely detest that kind of attention. I've never had any taste of it because the paparazzi don't appear to see classical performers as part of their work."

He acknowledges that the press pack game isn't always one-way traffic. Some celebrities are happy to crash with it head on.

"The perception that the public have of celebrities is something that comes with the territory of celebrity, especially the high profile artists," he says. >

Sitting in his understated, monotone backstage room at St David's Hall, Cardiff, Bryn reveals that Terry Morris's desire to recapture some of David Bailey's '60s spirit sits comfortably with him.

> "It depends if you're looking out for that kind of publicity. If you've got an album to sell, you're going to use it to your advantage.

"Living at the centre of such a cultural movement wouldn't be the first choice for anyone, I think, and when people don't want the publicity, it can be a problem. It's quite a balancing act."

Celebrity may bring with it selfish reasons for publicity but it can also bring a range of surprise benefits.

Bryn says, "I don't think I'd have had the confidence to start a festival in North Wales had I not seen other people succeed in Wales. It's frightening to put on something like Faenol because it costs well in excess of a million pounds.

"In the past 20 years the whole principality has developed and I think the '90s Cool Cymru thing was a catalyst for that. It's nice for the country and its people to have some confidence." ■

"In the past 20 years the whole principality has developed and I think the '90s Cool Cymru thing was a catalyst for that. It's nice for the country and its people to have some confidence."

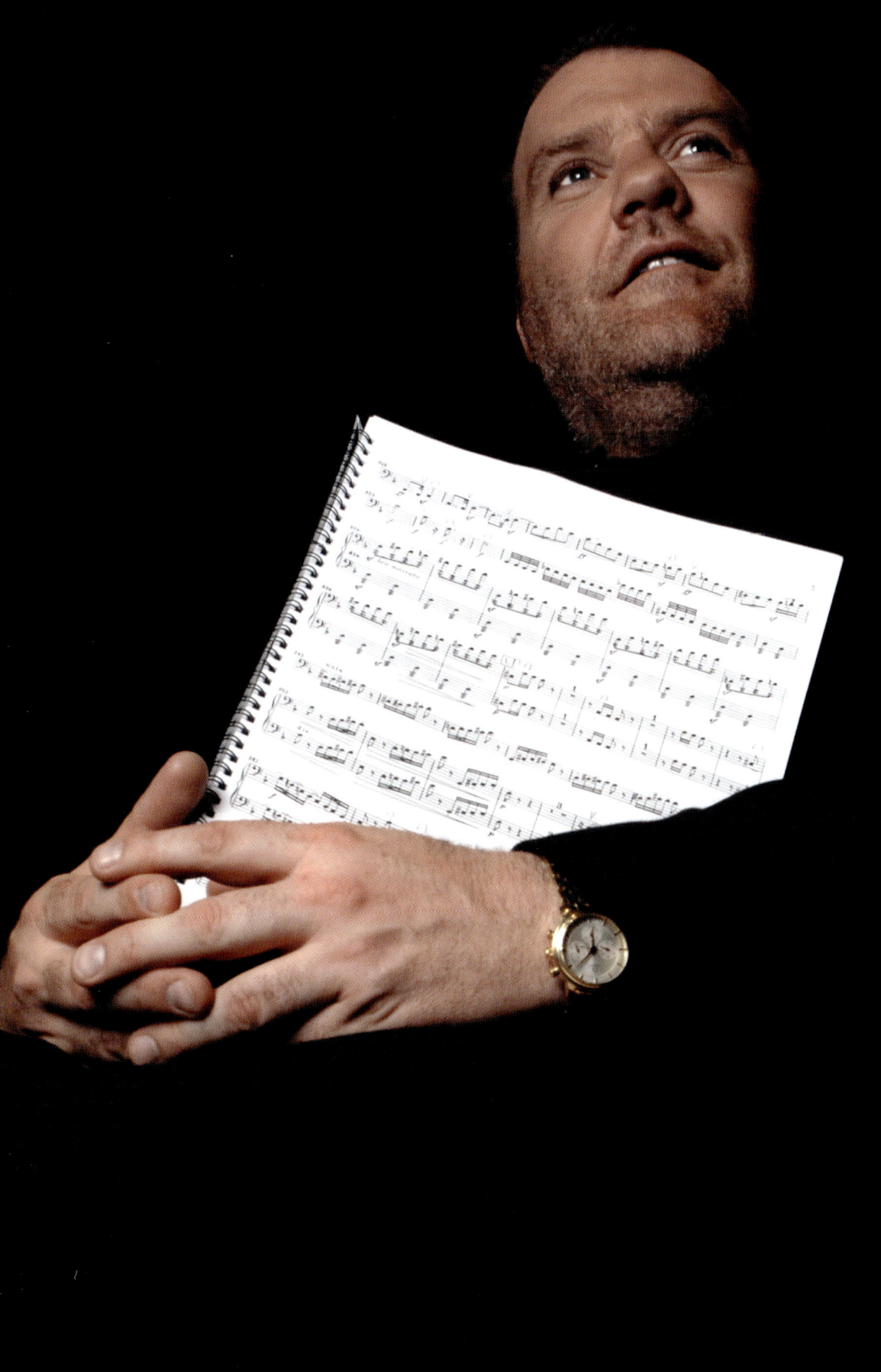

Hall of Fame
Fact File

- Bryn Terfel was born in 1965.

- Early performances included those in tents around Wales in youth culture festivals, the Urdd Eisteddfodau. (www.100welshheroes.com)

- The musical public at large caught their first glimpse of this future superstar at the 1989 Cardiff Singer of the World competition — even though he came second to another baritone, the Russian Dmitri Hvorostovsky. (www.100welshheroes.com)

- Bryn Terfel made his operatic debut with Welsh National Opera in 1990. He sang Guglielmo in Mozart's Cosi Fan Tutte.

A man and his music.

Ryan

Giggs

Ryan Giggs Setting the scene

Thursday, May 4, 2006

MANCHESTER United's main training complex oozes excellence. Fine-tuned professionalism glints from every blade of grass, every pane of glass.

Yet its discreet presence on the northern landscape belies its role as a home to superstars.

It nestles down a tree-lined lane in the Carrington countryside, a few miles south west of Manchester city centre. Tall trees shield whatever buildings lie within. The first-time visitor is given no hint of what rests inside.

Its entrance isn't signalled by flashing neon but by a small white sign. It reads: "Important notice. Due to dealers profiteering from the sale of signed memorabilia via the internet etc, the players will no longer sign footballs or shirts etc. We apologise to our genuine supporters."

A few yards away is a notice planted in a field that may or may not belong to United. Its instruction seems strange considering the type of business United have become so good at. "Private land," it says. "No shooting."

There's a remotely operated single bar security barrier.

A car driver noses up to the barrier. The motorist reaches out of his window and presses a button on a small speaker box. There's a mumble from the other end.

"It's Terry Morris," says the driver. "I'm here to take a photo of Ryan Giggs."

Before Terry finishes his sentence the barrier is rising.

Another narrow lane beckons, this time made of giant concrete slabs. It could be the route to a secret military base.

Lighting man Graham Harries spots the first sign of significant architecture.

"It's like a spaceship," he announces. "It's got a big fence all around it — and it looks like a spaceship."

The large, hangar-like structure features elegant lines thanks to banana-shaped exterior roof trusses. Thousands of light grey panels form the wall.

Once beyond a security booth, a smart, unhurried reception desk and a warm greeting from United facilities manager Clive Snell, Terry's inside the spaceship.

It turns out to be the main building of the club's academy, which nurtures young, developing talent.

It rises between a dozen or so pancake-flat training pitches — some complete with advertising hoardings — and a full-size AstroTurf training pitch.

Inside it's as clean as a referee's whistle and is fitted out smartly but with a determined functionality. Make no doubt about it, this may look like a sports complex built by Hilton — but it's a sports complex nonetheless.

Quietly, it exudes pride at the club's achievements over the years.

Upstairs, above an unfussy reception desk, is an airy milling area full of high-grade canteen tables and chairs. It's where parents gather when ferrying their offspring here for coaching sessions and games.

Leading from the reception is a central corridor, which separates changing rooms on one side from medical >

Lighting man Graham Harries spots the first sign of significant architecture. "It's like a spaceship," he announces. "It's got a big fence all around it — and it looks like a spaceship."

> suites, more changing rooms and a light-flooded structure which houses a full-size outdoor AstroTurf pitch. It's a breathtaking vision, an example of how today's major sports clubs must speculate to accumulate.

The senior players have something similar.

On the walls of the corridor are information boards featuring United heroes. They include big names like George Best, Mark Hughes, Gary Neville and Paul Scholes.

There are 9ft tall images of four United greats: David Beckham, Bobby Charlton, Duncan Edwards and Ryan Giggs.

In fact, Ryan is everywhere. His face appears on pictures of FA Youth Cup winning teams, FA Cup winning groups and on images that capture the glory of other memorable victories.

One member of the Carrington staff reveals, "Giggs the player is a legend among the footballers here — and the training ground staff. He's a good man as well."

One information board reads: "If there's passion in your heart and magic in your feet, success is in your grasp."

A fruitful career of almost two decades at the top suggests that Ryan has it all — the passion, the magic and the success. But what's he going to be like to photograph? ◼

One member of the Carrington staff reveals, "Giggs the player is a legend among the footballers here — and the training ground staff. He's a good man as well."

Ryan Giggs

Manchester United FC's Trafford Training
Centre, Carrington, Manchester
Thursday, May 4, 2006

Ryan Giggs The thought process

Thursday, May 4, 2006

NUMBERS can say as much as words. Just ask a sports statistician. Or a bookie.

A glance at www.manutd.com, the official Manchester United website, following the club's final game of the 2005–06 season, reveals a collection of notable figures.

Two numbers stand next to the name Ryan Giggs. The figure 672 signifies the number of occasions the Welshman has played for United during a fabulous career. The other — 134 — indicates how many goals he's scored.

The closest existing clubmate to rival Ryan's appearances total is Gary Neville — more than 160 games behind on 507.

Only one man has more goals — the prolific specialist striker Ruud Van Nistelrooy on 150.

Indeed, Ryan is one of only three men to have played more than 600 games for United. Bill Foulkes and Sir Bobby Charlton are the others.

Photographer Terry Morris, however, is attracted by one of football's more modest numbers. As United facilities manager Clive Snell explains the layout of the Carrington academy complex, he leads Morris 60 or 70 yards to the end of the main building's spinal corridor.

It's well lit and is lined with motivational panels highlighting past United glories and heroes. It features a series of rich red doors, each bearing 7ft-tall numbers in bright white. They start at 1 and end at changing room number 11.

"That's Giggsy's shirt number isn't it?" says Terry. "He has that for Man U and for Wales. I bet he's never been photographed in front of that door. That's got to be the picture."

As Clive departs, Terry asks lighting man Graham Harries to pose in the door for a series of test shots. He likes them — but is keen that the Ryan shot will possess one or two more eye-catching features.

"Giggs always looks so intense and focused when he's photographed in action," says Terry. "I'd like something completely different — a man relaxing and happy to be relaxed. A big beaming smile would be great."

The relaxation theme is to be accentuated by Ryan's dress for the shoot. He has agreed to wear a traditional black dinner suit and crisp white shirt.

It's in this impeccably fitted outfit, in punishing bright sunshine, that he glides across the car park from the first team training facility. He's lean and, with a perfect dark complexion, refreshingly handsome.

His close cropped, dark brown hair is showing glints of silver at the temple.

He's relaxed and wholly attentive as Terry explains what he plans to do.

First up is an icebreaker photo, a default image that will be used in the hall of fame if the shot outside dressing room 11 fails to work out.

In dressing room two, Terry has set up a clothes rail carrying four Manchester United jerseys, turned with their backs to the camera. Each says, "Giggs 11."

At the opposite end of the rail are four Wales shirts, in similar formation and in simlar vibrant red.

The footballer happily sits between >

Terry set up a clothes rail carrying four Manchester United jerseys turned with their backs to the camera. Each said, "Giggs 11." Opposite them were four Wales shirts in similar formation and in a similar vibrant red.

> them on a wall-mounted bench and leans forward in a number of poses.

But it's out in the corridor that things take a more dynamic shape. Standing in the doorway, Ryan takes on a more natural pose, even when asked to swap his black shoes for a pair of silver and red Reebok football boots.

Terry asks, "Ever had your picture taken in front of that door?"

He gets the answer he wants. "No," says Ryan. "A lot of places — but not here. I think you've got a first." ■

Terry's photo shoot in Manchester was aided by TV camera crew experts who helped with Ryan Giggs's styling.

Ryan Giggs agreed to wear a traditional black dinner suit and crisp white shirt. It was an impeccably fitted outfit.

Ryan Giggs The interview

Thursday, May 4, 2006

WHILE Terry Morris prepares to meet Ryan Giggs, there's a lengthy, sophisticated photo shoot going on a goal kick away.

Photographers from sportswear giant Nike have set up a studio in the Manchester United academy's indoor training barn. They're making good use of the covered full-size AstroTurf pitch.

Young Portuguese star Cristiano Ronaldo, England hero Rio Ferdinand and South Korean player Ji-sung Park are being ushered in to pose for today's shoot. It involves a creative team of many, with numerous tripod-mounted cameras catching each pose at varying angles.

It's top secret. Nike don't want information about the new strip leaking out before its high-profile public launch. Morris's small team are asked to steer clear — although some do manage to tuck into the Nike team's buffet laid out in the building's milling area. In their defence, they had been led to believe the food was a guest facility laid on by United.

With a nod toward the Nike people, Ryan is asked: "You must be pleased you're just doing Terry's shoot instead of all that."

The footballer returns a rueful smile. "I did it yesterday," he says. "It was all fine — they know their stuff."

Such attention is all in a day's work for a sports icon.

"Players here need to do photo shoots for United and the club's sponsors," says Ryan. "The sponsors of individual players also need to be kept happy.

"But all that's done in a controlled environment and the more you do, the more comfortable you get. I'm comfortable with that now."

He also appreciates that photography retains power as an art form.

He says: "I think photographers in that field should try to be as original as they possibly can. I always feel that those type of images work really well when they're black and white — that effect always seems to create an extra edge."

On the pitch it's the images of natural emotion and raw effort that capture his attention.

He says: "The ones that stick in the mind tend to be those that aren't staged.

"They might be of a goal celebration ... or maybe they show you shaking hands with someone you've just been trying to kick for 90 minutes!"

He has little time for playing the paparazzi game.

"That's something I'm not comfortable with," he says.

Privacy remains important. He says: "My life's split into contrasting parts. It's hectic when I'm playing football, training hard every day and getting involved in the intensity of preparing for games — but away from that I'm quite chilled, quite relaxed.

"I like going home and relaxing."

With a smile, he adds: "I've got a little girl who takes up most of my time ... although I wouldn't say that's relaxing until it's gone eight o'clock and she's in bed.

"It's different when a photographer's chasing you in circumstances you can't control — say you're just walking along the street or shopping. I don't think that's something you can be comfortable with.

"I've been lucky because I only really had that sort of attention when I was 18 to 22. After that I tried to keep myself to myself.

"As a footballer I don't see a need to play that game. As a footballer it's what you do out on the pitch that's important — you don't need to elaborate in other ways." ■

Hall of Fame Fact File

· Ryan Giggs was born in 1973.

· He moved to Manchester, aged seven, when his father signed to play rugby league for Swinton.

· He signed schoolboy forms with United aged 14, turned professional in 1990 and went on to win the FA Cup, the Premiership and the European Champions League to become the most decorated player in the club's history.

· Giggs made his debut for Wales when he came on as a substitute against West Germany in 1991. He has since won more than 50 caps.

Rhys

Ifans

Rhys Ifans Setting the scene

Wednesday, May 17, 2006

IT was an uncomfortable night for Terry Morris. The photographer was aching badly after an arduous, hot day putting down foundations for his house extension — and late on he was left considering a swift change of tack regarding his Rhys Ifans photo.

The labouring saw him rake, level and compact 10 tonnes of chippings and hardcore. He covered this with four inches of polystyrene insulation, put down an awkward plastic damp-proof membrane then oversaw the pouring of a five-inch layer of concrete from a ready-mix truck.

As the concrete layer levelled off to his satisfaction, a phone call revealed that Rhys was available to take his place in Terry's Welsh hall of fame. But the actor was on a tight schedule and had requested one key limitation to the shoot. There were to be no pictures that tried to be funny.

"Everything was hurting by the end of yesterday — especially the back," says Terry after breakfast, as he leaves Llanelli on an M4 drive up to Cardiff.

"The phone call was welcome but it scuppered my vision of the shoot. I'd wanted to do something quirky and had even bought a new toilet pan so I could get him sitting on it, trousers down, with a newspaper in front of him.

"I guess that's out now and, along with the physical aches, it did cause me to struggle with sleep. I suddenly had to re-think."

The new loo remains in a dark corner of his 101-year-old semi, currently undergoing an ambitious renovation. The original photo idea is on the spike.

Last night's phone call had come from Catrin Mears, of Merlin Marketing and Public Relations, who had been trying to arrange the photo shoot.

"Part of the feedback I had from Catrin was that Rhys wanted nothing comic," says Terry with a philosophical smile. "He's still often seen as that fella in the underpants in Notting Hill — but that was seven years ago, and now he's trying to shake off the lingering image of a joker. I know he's a good serious actor so I can understand if he's sick to death of photographers asking him to get his kit off.

"I'm comfortable with what he's asked. The most important thing is that we've got him and that we'll get a picture. It's my job to make sure it's a good one."

Catrin's call, with Terry in battered old jeans, a bruised T-shirt and well-worn wellies, had provided a moment of delicious contrast. One teatime Terry is physically shattered and in desperate need of a good shower; the next morning he's preparing to photograph a silver screen actor who's played alongside glamorous individuals such as Reese Witherspoon, Julia Roberts and Cate Blanchett.

The humour, however, is lost on Terry. He's just happy that his hall of fame is coming together and that the same can now be said of his home's new portrait studio and office space, together with a dressing room and en-suite for his master bedroom.

He says, "I didn't automatically think of me in my builder's glad rags one day then suddenly being thrust into the company of a film star.

"When Catrin called it was the cherry on top of the day. The hard work had been done - I'd finally got the foundations down so I could get on with the rest of the extension. Then I get a call saying the hall of fame will be taking a big step forward.

"I just went straight into picture mode. After the joy of getting the concreting done it was, 'Oh my God, what am I going to do tomorrow?'

"I didn't sleep well because I was thinking about what I could do. My mind was churning over with ideas. All sorts of things were going through my mind, and I soon forgot about the concrete. Sometimes when you've got a picture to take, you can think too much about it — and that's what started happening last night."

Eventually, Terry convinced mind and body that the best option was sleep. In Cardiff, things would take their own course and the shoot would be a success, he promised himself.

"All I've put in the Land Rover today is my camera, a light and a white backdrop," says Terry. "I know I'm going to be restricted by time and location — it'll just be 20 minutes in an office at Merlin — but we'll see what happens.

"Whatever looks good in the time I've got with Rhys will do me just fine."

He skirts Cardiff's most built-up areas and he parks at Merlin's wharf-side offices near the city centre. He carries out his equipment, meets Catrin and is led into the company's businesslike boardroom.

It might be plain except for a plasma TV, a number of framed images, some drinks making equipment and a large table — but it'll provide all the inspiration Terry will need. ▪

Rhys Ifans

Merlin Marketing and
Public Relations, Cardiff
Wednesday, May 17, 2006

Rhys Ifans

  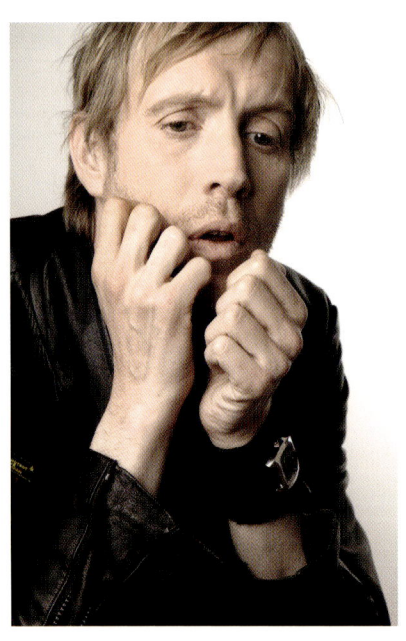 

For five minutes Rhys Ifans morphed his hands and face into a film strip of expressions, all coming through the eyes, mouth, a curl of the fingers and a ruffle of the hair. It was a remarkable lesson in the actor's art. The only noise in the room was the click of the camera.

Rhys Ifans The thought process

Wednesday, May 17, 2006

RHYS Ifans and the Super Furry Animals go back a long way. Tap them both into Google and you're told that the actor once meant more to the Welsh rock band than just a pal who has helped out with video filming.

BBC Online asks the question, "Did Rhys Ifans really once sing in the band?"

Helpfully, the corporation also supplies an answer.

"He did, but the band was very different at the time," you're told. "When they started, Super Furry Animals were a loose collective playing techno. The one-time Notting Hill star joined them for a short time on vocals, before the lure of prancing about on screen in his pants became too much to resist. Ifans also used to live with Daf from the band."

So, as photographer Terry Morris waits to meet Ifans on a warm lunchtime in Cardiff Bay, the word is that he's been in the company of SFA members who are working in the city and pleased to have the actor on board for a few days.

But Terry is focused on only one thing —

today's photographic job at the Cardiff headquarters of Merlin Marketing and Public Relations.

"I've decided on a really strong, tight head shot," he says. "I've had some time to think because setting up at Merlin only took five minutes — white backdrop, light, camera check and that was it. Some of Merlin's people helped me move a big table out of the room and I then got a low stool in there — chrome legs, simple black plastic seat.

As Rhys strolls out of the Eli Jenkins pub, he's unshaven, dressed in baggy blue hipster jeans, a lived-in dark leather jacket, T-shirt and black baseball boots.

He's never met Terry but greets him in friendly fashion as he hops into the photographer's Land Rover. He is taken on a short drive to Merlin HQ.

The only other people in the makeshift Merlin studio are Maria Evans, a make-up specialist Terry has commissioned for his hall of fame jobs, and the PR firm's Catrin Mears.

He tells Rhys about the project and asks the actor for some honest feedback as

he lays a number of large-scale prints on the floor. For two minutes there's silence, as Rhys looks carefully over the shots. It's a period of uncertainty for the photographer, awaiting judgement.

When Rhys looks up, however, it's clear that the photographer has nothing to worry about. The actor says, "They're great, Terry. This shot of my mate is like nothing I've ever seen of Bryn Terfel. All the pictures of him I've seen are in quite stuffy opera-style — in his tux — but you've captured Bryn as he is. He's a lovely bloke with a great smile. This is a refreshing take on him."

He also particularly likes the mysterious composition of the Charlotte Church image, with the singer behind a curtain of water. He enjoys the flash of red which makes the Ryan Giggs image leap from the photographic paper.

He says, "It's refreshing to see that the image consultants have been put to one side on all these and that the photographer has been allowed to develop his own ideas.

"Whatever picture of me you choose should be the one you keep in the collection. I'd love to see it when you decide — but whatever I think, you stick to your choice."

Rhys settles onto his stool and the shoot begins. Terry says he'd like "something serious, something different, an expression, a look."

He says, "I'm looking for a thoughtful image because a portrait like this will only be strong if the photographer gets something from the sitter — the sitter needs to give something."

Rhys considers the request, sinks his face into his hands and creates another two minutes of silence. This is broken when he asks, "Are you ready, Terry?"

"Yes," comes the reply.

"So am I," says Rhys … and he's off.

For five minutes the actor morphs his hands and face into a film strip of expressions, all coming through the eyes, mouth, a curl of the fingers and a ruffle of the hair. It's a remarkable lesson in the actor's art. The only noise in the room is the click of the camera. Terry captures around 40 distinct looks.

The end comes as Rhys makes a throat-

slitting gesture with a hand and says, "That's your lot. Have you got what you need?"

The photographer has. "That was brilliant," he says.

Terry shows Rhys the images on the camera screen. The actor smiles.

"Can I ask what you were thinking?" asks Terry.

"That's between me," smiles Rhys, "… and my shrink." ▪

Hall of Fame Fact File

- Rhys Ifans was born in 1968, with the name Evans.

- His family moved from Haverfordwest, Pembrokeshire, to Ruthin, Clwyd, when he was young. He attended Mold's Ysgol Maes Garmon.

- Early films included Swansea-based 1997 dark comedy Twin Town, in which he starred with brother Llyr Evans.

- Ifans won a Bafta best actor award in 2005 for his portrayal of comic Peter Cook in TV drama Not Only But Always.

Dame Shirley

Bassey

Dame Shirley Bassey Setting the scene

Friday, June 16, 2006

THE bacon butties in the Daubeny snack bar are hitting the spot for photographer Terry Morris and his lighting man Graham Harries. The bread has been cut thick, the meat is juicy. It's a late breakfast treat.

Yet the sandwiches seem at odds with the Chelsea Harbour ethos. Across the concourse are fine fabric businesses GP and J Baker, and Turnell and Gigon.

The former's wares include 'luxurious silks and rich textural weaves', the latter deals in fabrics, trimmings and wallpapers that range from the traditional to the startlingly contemporary.

Nearby is home furnishings outlet Donghia, specialising in bespoke, hand-built furniture and unique handmade wall coverings.

Next to the snack bar is Harbour Food and Wine. Being opposite the Chelsea Harbour Design Centre, this is no ordinary corner shop. Its magazine racks carry titles such as Grafik, Objekt, Creative Review and Design Week.

Other prominently displayed journals suggest that the harbour's residents don't have the humble bacon sandwich at the top of their snacking list. There's Vogue, Harper's Bazaar, Tatler, Homes Worldwide, Homes Overseas and the Robb Report Vacation Homes.

The wine cabinets feature much champagne — Veuve Clicquot Ponsardin, Joseph Perrier, Laurent-Perrier, Guy Cadel and Moet and Chandon. A bottle of '95 Dom Perignon will set you back £85, a '99 Louis Roederer £115.

Three minutes walk away is the marina, developed from former coal trade moorings in the late 1980s and now a permanent and temporary home to the well-off.

A typical two-bedroom river-view flat has an asking price of £1.25million — although you do get a 24-hour concierge with that.

Around 50 leisure boats are moored here, impeccably kept and some suitable for a large family. The whites and silvers glint in the strong morning sunshine. Monte Carlo resident Dame Shirley Bassey would approve.

Beyond the Belvedere — a 20-storey wizard-hat-topped tower of luxury apartments — is the Thames. In the near distance to the left is five-span wrought iron and steel Battersea Bridge. To the right — and much closer — is the 133-year-old Wandsworth Railway Bridge.

Private balconies in the harbour are bursting with floral colour. Parked at marina-side are a black Porsche and a red Ferrari. Hotel guests are taking coffee on the terrace of the extensive five-star Conrad Hotel. It advertises itself as a place close to the action of The King's Road, Sloane Square, Chelsea, Harrods and Knightsbridge.

If you made a list of words plucked from one of its brochures, it could include all of the following: style, comfort, space, luxury, style, state-of-the-art, delectable, modern, elegant.

A day's B&B for two this time next week is quoted on the hotel website as starting at around £250.

It's 10.15am and, in the Daubeny, Terry and Graham have finished their butties. Staff from businesses such as lighting specialist Bella Figura and home >

Private balconies in the harbour are bursting with floral colour. Parked at marina-side are a black Porsche and a red Ferrari.

> accessory specialist Porta Romana are back at work.

The two Welshmen make their way to the first floor of the harbour's Chambers (South) building and into office suite 112, last occupied by survey and mapping technologies business, Astrata.

The welcoming waft of unsoiled tufted loop pile greets the pair as they enter the six-room unit that has little other than carpets and blinds. The electrics are fine and there's ample room in the main room to create a studio. One vacated office will become a changing room for Dame Shirley.

Chairs and tables are borrowed from adjoining offices to make this room comfortable for the guest. Refreshments are prepared. Dame Shirley has asked for still water, tea, Canderel sweetener, lemon, fruit, biscuits and Cheddar cheese. The food and drink is positioned on a side table with crockery and cutlery borrowed from neighbouring rooms.

Over the next three hours there's much work to be done. Men from a conference installation firm bring a soft floor covering, large black drapes which will act as a backdrop to the photo shoot, and a large black felt floor covering. It's Terry's blank canvas and it must be brushed and vacuumed to clear away dust.

Also brought in are three domestic internal doors and frames. Terry has painted them white at home in Llanelli and there's great interest from the installation men as to how they're going to be used.

Terry and Graham position the doors in the middle of the black flooring. They're in a stepped formation, the nearest being on the right as Terry's lens will aim.

Graham runs a vacuum cleaner over part of the black floor and gets the thumbs up from Terry. A chauffeur-driven Mercedes carrying Dame Shirley is due to arrive at 2pm. ▪

Graham runs a vacuum cleaner over part of the black floor and gets the thumbs up from Terry. A chauffeur-driven Mercedes carrying Dame Shirley is due to arrive at 2pm.

Dame Shirley Bassey

Chelsea Harbour, London
Friday, June 16, 2006

Terry Morris scatters diamonds loaned by jeweller Asprey onto the floor of his makeshift Chelsea Harbour studio.

Terry makes a small adjustment to Dame Shirley Bassey's dress.

Cool Cymru Collection

Members of an ITV Wales film crew look on as Terry Morris and Dame Shirley Bassey talk ideas.

Let's see what we've got here. Dame Shirley has a sneak preview of her pictures.

Terry Morris and Dame Shirley Bassey in office suite 112 of Chelsea Harbour's Chambers (South) building.

Shining star Dame Shirley Bassey has enjoyed
more than half a century of showbiz success.

Dame Shirley Bassey The thought process

Friday, June 16, 2006

TERRY Morris is sipping from a chilled litre bottle of Evian as he awaits the arrival of his latest photographic subject.

He's in the heart of one of London's most exclusive locations, Chelsea Harbour, and has just finished transforming a suite of six unfurnished, unoccupied offices into a makeshift, remarkably together looking, studio.

He's reading up on Dame Shirley Bassey's singing career. A few web page printouts outline a story of longevity in a fickle industry.

"It says here that she started her career in 1953," says Terry. "That's 53 years ago — unbelievable. How can she have stayed so popular and so much on top of her game for so long?

"I'm just glad I've got a decent idea for this photo to reflect how she's kept going."

Terry has put up three white doors in their frames on a black floor cloth. On three sides are floor-to-ceiling black felt drapes. In front of this scene is Terry's photographic equipment — lights, umbrella-shaped reflectors and Nikon camera.

On the black floor, just in front of the doors, are around 300 diamonds. They are worth more than £1million.

They have been loaned by New Bond Street business Asprey. Sitting on a small chair near Terry is the jeweller's Genevieve Macleod. She is clutching a box that carries a diamond necklace and earring suite, together worth £96,000. They're on loan too, for Dame Shirley to wear during the shoot.

Dame Shirley's Twickenham-based hair and make-up artist Nikki Hambi arrives in good time, setting up in an office converted for use as the singer's changing room.

And right on time Dame Shirley arrives, a large, soft black cap being a focal point. Two people she knows from charity work with the Children's Hospital for Wales greet her — they are Lyn Jones and Suzanne Mainwaring.

Lyn is the chairman of trustees with the Noah's Ark Appeal. Suzanne is the appeal's director.

Dame Shirley is introduced to Terry and exchanges kisses on the cheek. She's quickly into her changing room where she chats with Nikki, Lyn, Suzanne and Terry.

The photographer reappears 15 minutes later with good news.

"The theme of today's picture is Diamonds Are Forever," he says. "Dame Shirley says that it's a first — it's never been done before, with all these diamonds. I'm really pleased."

After an hour with Nikki, the singer emerges from her room and fills the studio with chat. She's eager to give Terry her full commitment for the next hour.

Dame Shirley's eyes light up as she sees that Terry has arranged for the diamonds to be part of the shoot.

"My goodness," she laughs. "You shouldn't have got real ones. My big toe will come out and scoop one up — I've trained my big toe well!

"You could get paranoid with all these diamonds — is big brother watching?" >

The shooting with Dame Shirley took 45 minutes, Terry capturing many frames filled with the doors he'd shipped in to Chelsea from Llanelli.

Dame Shirley's eyes light up as she sees that Terry has arranged for the diamonds to be part of the shoot.

"My goodness," she laughs.
"You shouldn't have got real ones.
My big toe will come out and scoop one up — I've trained my big toe well!"

Terry Morris and Dame Shirley Bassey.

> However, she declines the opportunity to wear the £75,000 necklace, described by Asprey as a platinum diamond piece comprising 13 sections, each with two rows of six claw-set brilliant cut diamonds spaced by five baguette type diamonds.

"Oh that's beautiful — very nice," she says. "But I can't wear it because it wouldn't go with the dress being on just one shoulder."

She is happy to sport the Asprey earrings, a £21,000 pair featuring a total of 66 diamonds.

"The earrings are lovely," she purrs. "And they're mine — for the moment at least!"

She's happy that the doors represent her career's past, present and future — the one for the past is open, the one for the present is ajar and the one for the future is closed.

Terry tells her, "We know it'll open soon — and, who knows, it might stay open forever. That's why we've got all these diamonds. Diamonds are forever"

The shooting starts and it goes on for 45 minutes, Terry capturing many frames filled with the three doors, Dame Shirley looking sexy and mysterious in her black Vivienne Westwood dress.

The images improve when Terry's right-hand man Graham Harries places a gold-coloured star on each door. Terry had crafted them from card at home. He closes in on the singer and gets a number of close-ups that please him.

The gems scattered on the floor are now out of the frame — £1million seems an awful lot of diamonds to discard.

It may be that they won't be wasted. When Terry returns home to Llanelli, he'll study his images from today and decide which one will have most impact in his hall of fame. ■

Dame Shirley looked sexy and mysterious in her black Vivienne Westwood dress.

Dame Shirley Bassey The interview

NOT for the first time in a career of more than half a century, Dame Shirley Bassey is big news.

Journalists covering a high profile royal event yesterday were delighted that the singer inadvertently supplied them with a strong, humorous angle amongst all the stage-managed pomp.

The occasion — to help mark the Queen's 80th birthday celebrations — was a national service of thanksgiving at St Paul's Cathedral. Among the guests were 42 members of the Royal Family, including the Duke and Duchess of Gloucester, and the Earl and Countess of Wessex.

Some news providers reported that Dame Shirley's Audi had screeched to a halt outside St Paul's shortly before the arrival of the Queen's Bentley.

"Just seconds before the Queen's arrival, latecomer Dame Shirley Bassey sneaked into a side door of the cathedral," reported pipex.com.

Some would have been thrown by such attention. Not Dame Shirley. Indeed, she's full of life as she enters Chelsea Harbour the day after her scrape with tardiness.

As she dashes into suite 112 of the harbour complex's Chambers (South) block, she greets photographer Terry Morris. She sweeps into her changing room and talks to Terry with great animation.

"Oh my goodness, you'll never guess what I did yesterday," she says. "I was almost late for the Queen! I got the times wrong — I arrived an hour after I should have — and made the news.

"I was pleased that the ushers at St Paul's were so good. They directed me straight to my seat and everything went really well."

The singer sees the humorous side to the incident. Indeed, shortly after the faux pas, she had the presence of mind to seek help for a man suffering in the powerful sunshine of the early afternoon.

She's keen to tell the story, which concerns a function that followed the cathedral event. It had been hosted by the City of London Corporation and its Lord Mayor, David Brewer.

"We all went back to the Mansion House for dinner," says Dame Shirley. "I noticed on my way in that one of the Lord Mayor's ceremonial bodyguard — in his lovely uniform — was feeling the effects of the heat. He looked like he was about to faint.

"I decided to call help because the least he needed was a glass of water — but by the time I'd caught sight of the poor man again he was being dragged away by some of his colleagues. My help had obviously been too late in coming."

Throughout the two hours she's in suite 112, Dame Shirley is in cheerful mood.

Terry shows her some shots he's already done for his Wales hall of fame. She particularly likes an image taken on stage at St David's Hall, Cardiff.

"Oh, Bryn Terfel, my lovely Bryn," she says. "I saw him in Tosca the other night and he was marvellous. I really loved it, every minute of it. I'm a fan of Tosca now, and I'll go back and back again to see it."

Terry, however, is out of earshot when she is asked about photography. "My favourite pictures are those that make me look absolutely gorgeous," she laughs. "I don't have a favourite photographer, but if I did it would be one that made me look good.

"Naturally, you don't want to look unattractive, so whatever photographer takes the best picture would be the one for me."

The singer may not study photography but she does seem to know how to relax away from the limelight.

Dame Shirley says, "In my spare time I go to the cinema, I go to the gym, I cook anything that keeps my mind occupied. I like to eat healthily — and a teatime treat would be caviar … with baked potato!" ▪

Hall of Fame Fact File

- Dame Shirley was born in 1937.

- Her 1957 debut single, The Banana Boat Song, reached the top 10.

- In 1964 she achieved chart success in the UK and America with Goldfinger, the theme to the James Bond film. Two further Bond themes followed — Diamonds Are Forever (1972) and Moonraker (1979).

- Occasional performances in Wales in recent years have included 1999's Assembly opening and the same year's Rugby World Cup appearance, singing World in Union with Bryn Terfel.

loan

Gruffudd

Ioan Gruffudd Setting the scene

Wednesday, August 2, 2006

BREAKFAST at the Best Western Sunset Plaza Hotel. It's 7.30am as Terry Morris sips fresh filter coffee from a plastic cup then pours milk into a pre-packed plastic bowl of Kellogg's Corn Flakes.

He's two-and-a-half hours away from photographing one of world cinema's brightest rising stars, but there's still much prep work to be done. Having found a hotel at 11pm last night, there's been little time for Terry and right-hand man Graham Harries to research and firm up locations.

It's a sprawling city out there — 470 square miles and around four million inhabitants — but all the pair have seen so far is the international airport, the inside of their hired Buick people mover and the night's roads between Alamo car rentals and the hotel.

"We've managed six or seven hours kip, but that came after a hastily arranged three-hour drive from Llanelli to Heathrow, a four-hour wait at the airport and an 11-and-a-half-hour flight," says Terry. "We knew we might get this chance only 48 hours ago. We're shattered but over the moon to be here.

We're in West Hollywood on the world-famous Sunset Strip and we've got a photo shoot at 10am with Ioan Gruffudd. Does it get any better than that?"

Overlooking the low-slung Best Western is the Sunset Tower Hotel, an art deco masterpiece designed in the late '20s and close to the strip's famous restaurants and clubs of the next few decades.

Former Sunset Tower residents include Howard Hughes, John Wayne, Marilyn Monroe, Errol Flynn, Elizabeth Taylor, Frank Sinatra and Truman Capote. It has appeared in films such as Get Shorty and was mentioned in Raymond Chandler's 1940 novel Farewell, My Lovely.

The Comedy Club is across the road, and a mile or so to the west is Beverly Hills.

It's an apt place to meet a leading man.

"Last night's drive here took a couple of hours because we had to spend time looking for a room," says Terry. "We tried a couple of fleapit motels but they stank, they had ants crawling up the walls and there were a few dodgy

characters knocking about. We didn't fancy being uncomfortable, or mugged."

The Sunset Boulevard accommodation they settled for is clean, tidy and secure. It has fine views of LA's high-rise business district, a few miles through the heat haze to the south.

The Best Western is a 10-minute stroll from the cinematic red, white and blue burst of retro neon that is Mel's Drive-in. It's a five-minute drive from a second possible photo shoot location — the all-American chrome and comfort zone of Frank Corrente's Cadillac Corner.

"We're right where we want to be but we're running on adrenalin," admits Terry. "We've still got to check with the drive-in and with the Cadillac place that we're free to use their premises for this job. If the people there say 'no' then it'll be a major rush to find somewhere equally photogenic and convenient. I'm looking for a great American setting, but I don't want to waste the limited time we'll have with Ioan — it's so brilliant of him to agree to spend an hour or so with us."

"We've left a phone message with >

Terry says, "We tried a couple of fleapit motels but they stank, they had ants crawling up the walls and there were a few dodgy characters knocking about. We didn't fancy being uncomfortable, or mugged."

> Frank Corrente, and the diner manager clocks on any minute now."

The pair leave the hotel, drive to Mel's and manoeuvre the Buick into a car park behind the diner. The duty manager says he has no problem with a photo shoot.

He points Terry in the direction of three tables overlooked by giant black and white prints of movie American Graffiti being filmed at Mel's original San Francisco base. The 1973 George Lucas rock'n'roll fable featured star names such as Ron Howard, Richard Dreyfuss and Harrison Ford.

Terry says that Mel's robust, tan leatherette pews and solidly built black tables are everything he could want of an American diner. The tables are topped with bottles of Heinz Ketchup — "America's favourite" — and Heinz Pourable Mustard. There are sachets of House Recipe Honey, from Houston, Texas, Smucker's Orange Marmalade, from Orrville, Ohio, and Knott's Berry Farm Seedless Boysenberry Jam, from Omaha, Nebraska.

Compact metal jukebox terminals on each table suggest an evocative movie soundtrack of their own. Choices include Count Basie's One O'Clock Jump, Glenn Miller's Moonlight Cocktail, Otis Redding's (Sittin' on) the The Dock of the Bay, Little Richard's Long Tall Sally and Roberta Flack's Will You Still Love Me Tomorrow? Elvis weighs in with Jailhouse Rock, Neal Hefti with the Batman Theme and Danny and the Juniors with At The Hop.

The tall, laminated menu cards offer some specials for breakfast. The El Rancho is described as a flour tortilla rolled with three scrambled eggs, chorizo and Cheddar cheese. It's topped with tomato salsa, tomatillo salsa and sour cream, and it's served with fruit or grilled potatoes.

As Terry settles into a pew, a phone call from the Cadillac place suggests that Frank Corrente likes the photographer's idea. Things are starting to slot into place.

However, the Welshman foregoes the El Rancho. He opts for a cappuccino and, in the shadow of George Lucas, awaits Ioan Gruffudd. ▪

As Terry settles into a pew, a phone call from the Cadillac place suggests that Frank Corrente likes the photographer's idea. Things are starting to slot into place.

Ioan Gruffudd

Frank Corrente's Cadillac Corner, Los Angeles
Wednesday, August 2, 2006

Ioan Gruffudd The thought process

IOAN Gruffudd's parents are enjoying a short break at his new Los Angeles home. He's intent on showing them a good time, and one highlight has been a brief but educational tour of California's vineyards.

Today, he must also fit in a couple of scheduled business meetings. Oh, and it's the birthday of his fiancé, the actress Alice Evans.

Nevertheless, one of Hollywood's most promising new talents turns up at Mel's Drive-in, on Sunset Boulevard, on the dot at 10am. He looks tall, slim and healthy.

He's never met photographer Terry Morris or lighting man Graham Harries but happily provides warm handshakes. His greetings are in Welsh and English. Dressed in pale red T-shirt, blue jeans and white tennis pumps, he slides comfortably into one of the diner's many pews. He orders a cappuccino.

Early banter revolves around life in the States. He tells Terry where to find LA's best Guinness, and talks of informal football sessions in the city with pals. >

Terry thought the robust, leatherette pews and solidly built tables at Mel's Drive-in were everything he could want of an American diner.

Terry explained to Ioan Gruffudd that he wanted a picture that instantly told the viewer it was taken in America. The actor liked the idea and sat for 20 minutes, posing with his large coffee mug.

> There's talk of Welsh rugby, especially a proposed move by the Llanelli Scarlets away from Stradey Park — their home for more than 125 years — to a purpose-built new stadium.

Ioan talks about his days as a junior rugby player, appearing with school teams and with Cardiff RFC teenage outfits. He was a full-back and recalls the days fondly.

But he's moved on, has made a big screen name for himself and is now being told by Terry that he is to appear in the photographer's Wales hall of fame collection.

Terry explains the concept and begins showing Ioan large prints of images already in the can. The actor likes them and enjoys seeing familiar faces in original settings.

"Oh, look at Rhys Ifans," he says. "He's a real character; incredibly talented; a brilliant actor.

"There's Stuart Cable, another character. I appeared in one of his TV shows and we got on well — we're from the same place, the Aberdare area.

"That's a nice picture of Gavin Henson; he looks like a caged animal. It's unfortunate there's so much attention on his life away from the rugby field. He should be allowed to get on with playing the game well.

"Oh, Bryn Terfel — I love that man! I know him from social functions over the years. Whenever we've been in Cardiff at the same time he's called to catch up.

"That's a good shot of Charlotte Church. It looks as if she's pulling two curtains aside. She's a real character and that's an amazing look; brilliant."

Terry explains that he wants a picture today that instantly tells the viewer it was taken in America.

The actor likes the idea and sits for 20 minutes, posing with his large coffee mug, a Mel's menu card promising "American food at its best," and the morning's edition of the Los Angeles Times. Headlines include, "Fighting Intensifies as Israel Pushes Farther Into Lebanon", "4 Latino Gang Members Are Convicted of Anti-Black Plot" and "More LAPD Sensitivity Training is Sought."

Terry's pictures look good on the screen of his Nikon but, bill settled and bags packed, Terry, Graham and Ioan hop into their cars and drive a mile or two east on Sunset. They pull up outside Frank Corrente's Cadillac Corner.

Last night, Terry spotted a 1950 white convertible Cadillac there. Its rich tan leather upholstery, glistening chrome and chunky push-button radio yell, "America!"

Terry chats with Frank who agrees to the photo shoot. The motor dealer starts the car and, with the engine providing a growl as deep as the Pacific, pulls it out onto Sunset. He parks it on the wide sidewalk.

"The heavier they are, the better they ride," purrs one of Frank's mechanics. "This one rides like a cloud."

The morning's grey and white clouds have cleared in the hot sun to reveal a brilliant blue sky.

For 20 minutes, Ioan poses with the car, sitting in front of it on the sidewalk then easing onto the driver's seat. >

The menu card at Mel's Drive-in promised Ioan Gruffudd "American food at its best."

They pull up outside Frank Corrente's Cadillac Corner. Last night, Terry spotted a 1950 white convertible Cadillac there. Its rich tan leather upholstery, glistening chrome and chunky push-button radio yell, "America!"

An American dream. The 1950 Cadillac used in Terry Morris's LA photo shoot.

The writing's on the wall as Terry Morris and Graham Harries talk technical matters.

Graham Harries films the LA photo shoot.

> Cars, trucks, buses and motorbikes rush by on one side of the car, a few semi-curious pedestrians shuffle by on the other.

Terry shows Ioan the results on his camera and both are delighted. The photographer reckons that the hall of fame collection will feature a Cadillac shot rather than the drive-in picture.

Ioan says, "I like the one in the car. It's got an iconic American thing going for it. There's no disputing it was taken in America and it's got a real timeless feel to it." ■

The scene: Sunset Boulevard, Los Angeles. The subject: One of Hollywood's most promising new talents.

Ioan Gruffudd through the windscreen.

Ioan says, "I like the one in the car. It's got an iconic American thing going for it. There's no disputing it was taken in America and it's got a real timeless feel to it."

At Frank Corrente's Cadillac Corner, a mechanic talked about the car chosen for the photo shoot. He said, "The heavier they are, the better they ride. This one rides like a cloud."

Ioan Gruffudd, Terry Morris and the 1950 Cadillac on the Sunset Boulevard sidewalk.

From left, Graham Harries, Terry Morris and Ioan Gruffudd outside
Frank Corrente's Cadillac Corner on Sunset Boulevard, Los Angeles.

Ioan Gruffudd The interview

Wednesday, August 2, 2006

A MOVE to the movie capital of the world has delighted Ioan Gruffudd. The young Welshman relocated to Los Angeles three years ago after a spell in London — and he loves it.

There's so much going on here that there's no excuse to get bored. The CityBeat entertainment newspaper is published every week, with thousands of ads and thousands of editorial column inches advising how best to spend your time.

This week's issue flags up a free music festival at the Henry Mancini Institute, two big concerts by the Los Angeles Philharmonic and weekend psychology programmes at the city's Antioch University.

There's the grand opening of "one of southern California's most respected yoga studios" and Virgin Megastores are hosting live events with actor Andy Garcia, singer Jody Whatley and the band Starsailor.

Eating out is a delight. There's everything from Brazilian steakhouses to Middle Eastern restaurants and from Creole joints to outposts of Japanese cuisine.

Down at the beach there are thousands of car parking places. Stalls specialise in hiring in-line skates. There are bikes of all shapes and sizes. Coastguard huts, as seen in TV's Baywatch, punctuate the miles of soft, golden sand.

If shopping's your thing then there's everything from outlets by the name of Trashy Lingerie to opulent new malls fronted by department store giants Macy's and Bloomingdale's.

The sightseeing business is thriving. One bus tour of stars' homes takes you to the LA residences of, amongst others, Robert Redford, Jennifer Lopez, Britney Spears, Leonardo DiCaprio and Jack Nicholson.

Movie openings have just taken place for The Ant Bully, with the voices of Nicolas Cage and Julia Roberts, and Miami Vice, featuring Colin Farrell and Jamie Foxx.

It's easy to understand why anybody planning a career in entertainment should be here.

And Ioan Gruffudd makes no apologies for his move. He's merely a man trying to do the best he can with his particular skills.

"I'm just putting myself into the middle of the biggest cauldron of my industry says Ioan. "That's why I'm here — and the bonus is that the weather's great, as is the lifestyle."

"I don't think you should begrudge anyone the chance to pursue a career. The best sports academies in the world are in Australia, so you wouldn't begrudge a move there for someone who'd like to be a swimmer. Similarly, there's every reason why a scientist should seek to go to the place where companies are developing the next important medicine.

"I think it's important to leave your home country, if you can, to explore the world. This can make you more rounded as a person and you'll carry the experience with you throughout your life, adding to your sense of identity and giving you extra confidence. You can get a bit stagnant if you remain in the same place."

Some LA lifestyle attractions come in categories usually classed as less exotic than weekend trips to Venice Beach.

Ioan says, "Ordinary things happen really quickly here, a lot quicker than >

"I'm just putting myself into the middle of the biggest cauldron of my industry," says Ioan. "That's why I'm here — and the bonus is that the weather's great, as is the lifestyle."

"I miss the people in Cardiff and London but I do love living in LA. The weather here makes you want to get out of bed every day to go and do something – and I'm in the heart of the industry I want to work in."

they sometimes happen back home.

"When I first moved here I was amazed by the speed some things were done. The gas was connected to the house straight away, and the cable TV guy wanted to come round and get things sorted the day after I'd called him. I'd never managed to get that job done in London.

"I miss the people in Cardiff and London but I do love living in LA. The weather here makes you want to get out of bed every day to go and do something — and I'm in the heart of the industry I want to work in."

As he prepares to leave Terry Morris following their Sunset Boulevard photo shoot, Ioan reveals that he's about to start filming on the sequel to 2005 comic book adventure The Fantastic Four.

It will mean several months in Canada, away from his new home.

He says, "I bought the house a few months ago and I love to relax outside by the Jacuzzi and little pool. The pool's not a very big one — you can't do laps in it — but it's lovely to chill out there. It's so nice to get up every day and jump in." ▪

Hall of Fame Fact File

- Ioan Gruffudd was born in 1973.

- He attended Ysgol Gymraeg Melin Gruffydd in Whitchurch, Cardiff, the nearby Ysgol Gyfun Gymraeg Glantaf and London's Royal Academy of the Dramatic Arts.

- Ioan appeared in Welsh TV soap Pobol y Cwm in the late '80s and early '90s. His big breakthrough came in the lead role of TV series Hornblower.

- Key film roles have included The Fantastic Four (2005), King Arthur (2004) and Titanic (1997).

Joe

Calzaghe

Joe Calzaghe Setting the scene

Thursday, August 24, 2006

THE library's closed in Abercarn. It is every Thursday. The steel concertina security doors are pulled across the main entrance and a tall green wheelie bin stands sentry on the pavement bordering High Street.

Up the road, the Commercial Inn's shut too, this lunchtime. An advertising board high on a wall offers those interested a chance to manage the pub. A blackboard around the corner, in Market Place, shouts, "Pool room open!" It also offers, "Jugs of vodka and Red Bull, £8."

Next door, the Market Tavern's cream walls promote only Carling. A few doors up the old, narrow street is the well tended Abercarn Workingmens' Club and Institute. Worthington Creamflow Bitter is advertised on a sign above its closed front door.

No-one's standing at the bus stop — there's no 151 to Newport or N2 to Crumlin due.

Photographer Terry Morris is here, halfway up the Ebbw Valley. He's looking for Newbridge Boxing Club where he has an appointment with a man who has

taken on the world — and won.

He's fascinated by the contrast between the hullabaloo surrounding Joe Calzaghe's previous fight, a stunning victory over great American hope Jeff Lacy, and the relative solitude of the champion's village base. Abercarn on a Thursday lunchtime is far removed from the Manchester MEN Arena on a big fight night.

The run-up to the world championship Lacy bout had seen the sport's seemingly traditional war of words, this time between Calzaghe promoter Frank Warren and his counterpart Gary Shaw.

In England's northern capital in the early hours of March 5 there were thousands of fans. Around the world, millions watched on TV. Everything associated with a Warren promotion was there, including News of the World sponsorship and a macho American fighter in silky red, white and blue shorts. There was blood, sweat, tears and noise.

Ringside seats had gone for hundreds of pounds. The Calzaghe name was writ large on the Welsh boxer's Everlast shorts.

It was, incredibly, Calzaghe's 18th successful defence of his title. Now, at the silent steps of Abercarn's war memorial, a few Remembrance wreaths have rolled to the ground, encouraged by a gentle breeze. There are offerings from the Scouts, the Royal British Legion, Abercarn and Newbridge Rotary Club, Risca Police Station and Caerphilly County Borough Council.

There's one from "Irene, Paul and Family, Chris, Keith and Family." The Royal Engineers have laid a wreath bearing their crest, as have REME, the Royal Electrical and Mechanical Engineers. It's dignified and moving. It shows that a million miles from fight night glitz, the passion for community remains in Wales's traditional valley settlements.

Terry Morris drives past shop fronts happily displaying home-made posters that confirm a thriving neighbourhood.

Newbridge Rugby Club is three days away from hosting a bank holiday music event featuring The Daggers and the November Criminals — "Tickets £5. Get them early or miss out!!!"

Auditions are being advertised for a >

Photographer Terry Morris is here, halfway up the Ebbw Valley. He's looking for Newbridge Boxing Club where he has an appointment with a man who has taken on the world – and won.

> local Christmas panto production of Beauty and the Beast, and in three weeks' time the congregation of St Tudor's Church, Mynyddislwyn, is to host a best-loved songs of praise service — "Sing along to your top 10 local favourites. Tickets £2, include refreshments." The same venue is about to host a service of animal blessing.

Abercarn RFC has just staged a night of soul and disco with The Dukes; villagers are being urged to attend a bank holiday family fun day in aid of cardiac care at Cardiff's Heath Hospital; and Valleys pop hero Ricky Valance (Tell Laura I Love Her) is about to present a Swinging '60s Night at the Newbridge Memo, with Shadows tribute act Shaboogie — "Tickets £8, first drink free (excluding spirits)."

One poster tells Terry that he's just missed another show at the Memo — live music with Ann Clayton, Omega 66 and the headliners, Captain Paranoid and the Delusions.

The photographer stops in High Street, opposite Tanfastic Leisure Sunbed Hire and Sales. He pops a question to a shopper.

"Any idea where the Calzaghe gym is, pal?" he asks.

The man, in tweed jacket, shirt and stripy tie, points to the main A467.

"Turn left into the main road," he says. "Take a quick right, a sharp left into the industrial estate and follow that road as it bears right and left. Straight in front of you there'll be a mobile burger van — it's open from eight in the morning till two most days. Park there, the gym's through the trees behind the van."

Terry's happy at the thought of parking next to a burger van. He's hungry. ▪

Terry stops in High Street, opposite Tanfastic Leisure Sunbed Hire and Sales. He pops a question to a shopper. "Any idea where the Calzaghe gym is, pal?" he asks. The man, in tweed jacket, shirt and stripy tie, points to the main A467.

Joe Calzaghe

Newbridge Boxing Club, Abercarn
Thursday, August 24, 2006

Joe Calzaghe The thought process

Thursday, August 24, 2006

THERE used to be a flourishing tinplate industry and ironworks scene in the Abercarn area. Not any more.

The Prince of Wales Colliery used to stand on the banks of the Ebbw River. It was the scene of a disaster in 1878, when explosions led to 258 deaths.

A plaque at the entrance to an industrial estate built on the site reads, "Badly burned and wounded men were brought to the surface. When all accessible survivors had been brought to the surface a momentous decision was taken by the managers. In order to quell the inferno raging underground, the waters of the nearby Monmouthshire Canal were turned into the mine and the workings were flooded from above, an act which meant certain death for anyone still in the mine.

"There was hardly a house in the village where death had not struck. Of the 258 men and boys, 136 were married with families."

Photographer Terry Morris pulls into a small Tarmac car park opposite the fire station. There's a small number of cars, along with two or three people taking advantage of a white mobile burger van, doing a useful lunchtime trade.

"Joe Calzaghe's place is meant to be behind these trees," says Terry, nodding at the mature woodland almost enshrouding the van.

He hops out of his Land Rover, finds there's a narrow rough lane that leads through the trees, and drives through.

The downhill track leads past an open single-bar security gate and soon opens out into a bumpy grit and cinder area used for parking.

Next to this stands a low-slung breeze block and pebble dash structure. It's dwarfed by its steep-sided, heavily wooded valley. It seems to be on only nodding acquaintance with the neighbouring recreation field that has rugby posts, a Subbuteo-sized area of covered terracing, and cricket sightscreens.

A large sign on one side of the breeze block building reveals that it used to be a clubhouse for a local rugby club. It reads, "Cwmcarn United RFC."

Another sign — hand-painted in black and cream by someone who may well not be a professional sign writer — says, "Newbridge Boxing Club."

Terry is greeted by a small, wiry man with a joke and a mock punch in the stomach. It's Joe's dad, Enzo, who — as trainer — has led the fighter to a world title and to numerous defences of that prize.

The photographer is ushered in and meets Joe, cooling down after training and now preparing for the photo shoot.

There's a pungent smell of rubber, plastic, sweat and old lino. Training tops hang on hooks in a corridor, training shoes sit on top of busy filing cabinets. Notices flutter on the walls as you walk past. One says, "Attention all boxers. When you are in the gym you need these things to be able to train or spar: 1. Wrist wraps; 2. Bag gloves or sparring gloves; 3. Gum shield; 4. Spare pair of trainers. Remember: Monday is pay day – £5."

Other posters are bigger and more dramatic. One features a shot of Sylvester Stallone as movie boxer Rocky Balboa. "Prepare for the fight of your life," it urges. It's an advert for >

Terry Morris first asked Joe Calzaghe to wear a smart black suit because he wanted to show that when the boxer gets into the ring he means business.

The main prop Terry Morris got for Joe Calzaghe was a large black and chrome barber chair, borrowed from the KH2 salon in Llanelli.

> Rocky: The Game.

The rugby club's former lounge is now home to a multi-gym and running machines. The area behind the bar, once patrolled by busy staff, is now a store for boxing paraphernalia such as gloves and tape.

The former function room, complete with stage and disused bar, is now the main gym. Punchbags hang from the ceiling like monster fruit bats. They're in various shapes, sizes and colours. Half the hall is taken up by a full-size boxing ring, complete with water buckets in two corners and jars of Vaseline to one side.

Terry is impressed.

"You can smell hard work," he says. "It's a gutsy type of gym. The whole place has a great atmosphere. There are no frills — Joe's obviously stuck to his roots.

"I wasn't expecting this. I was anticipating something a bit more modern or, dare I say it, up-market. But maybe this is why Joe's stood the test of time. It obviously works for him because he's been a world champion for going on a decade."

Around the gym walls are posters used to advertise some of Joe's fights. There are memories of defeated opponents such as Will "Kid Fire" McIntyre, Mark Delaney, David Starie and Spencer Alton.

Terry says, "It's nice that I'm coming to a place where a man feels really at home but where I'm going to ask him to do something quite alien to him.

"I'm going to get him out of his Everlast tracksuit and put him in a smart black suit because I want to show that, although he's a sportsman of the highest calibre, when he gets into the ring he means business.

"I've brought some suits and I fancy a pin-striped number like you might see in Vogue magazine — really up-market. We want to portray Joe as being right at the sharp end of his business."

Another prop he's got is a large black and chrome barber chair, borrowed from the KH2 salon in Llanelli.

Terry says, "I love its shape and the fact that when the flash goes, all the chrome lights up. It's well made and it looks expensive — you're looking at the best part of £2,000 to buy one.

"I hope Joe likes the idea." ▪

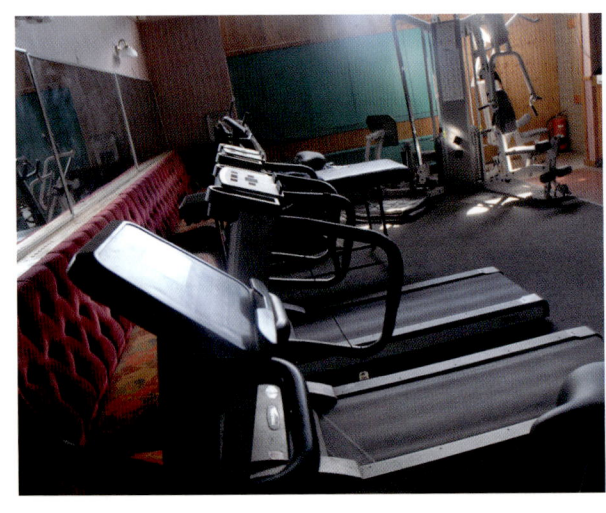

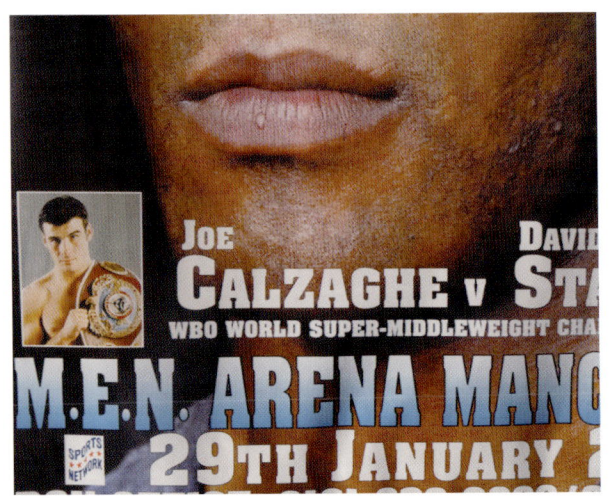

Joe Calzaghe faces up to his latest challenge – a photo shoot with Terry Morris.

Joe Calzaghe The interview

JOE Calzaghe's not the only man from the Newbridge area to have left his mark on modern culture.

Steve Strange took his group Visage to the top of the charts around the world in 1981 with Fade to Grey. Rugby heroes include forward Ray Cale, a union star with the Grand Slam-winning 1950 Wales side and a league success at St Helens.

Some who followed in Ray's footsteps at Cardiff Arms Park are still big draws on his old Newbridge patch. As Terry Morris prepares to meet Joe Calzaghe, Abercarn RFC is advertising a forthcoming gentlemen's evening with former British Lion Bobby Windsor. Less than a month later, ex-Wales star Steve Fenwick is booked to appear at a similar event in the nearby workingmens' club.

Joe recognises the importance of success to his community — and the importance of his community to those who're successful. He's happy that a pal such as James Dean Bradfield has tasted triumph with standard-bearing Welsh band the Manic Street Preachers.

"I went to the same local comprehensive school as the Manics. They've always followed my boxing and have been to a few fights, and I've followed them," he says. "It's great that such a small area can produce success that has an impact around Britain and around the world."

Joe believes that acts central to the 1990s Cool Cymru story, such as the Manics and Stereophonics, have had a positive lasting effect on Wales.

He says, "I like the music of that time. I know Kelly Jones and Stuart Cable from the Stereos — they're down to earth guys like myself. Like the Manics, we're all from a small country and we've all made our marks. It's great, putting Wales on the map.

"I keep my feet on the ground and still live in the area where I was brought up. I'm still proud to be Welsh."

But is it still cool to be Welsh?

"I don't know," says Joe, with a smile. "I suppose that if you're Welsh it is cool … and if you're not Welsh maybe you're not cool! Personally, I think it's great to be in Wales; I get a lot of pleasure from it."

He draws parallels between Wales and Sardinia, the home of his father and trainer, Enzo.

Joe says, "I'm half Sardinian and I know that the people there look on Italy in a similar way to how the Welsh look on England. Sardinians have their own heritage and their own distinct land — an island — so perhaps I've got a good mix due to those two places. Maybe I get my skills and strength from Wales and Sardinia."

His colleagues at Newbridge Boxing Club are also an essential factor in his glory.

He says, "The fighters here have all either got titles or are contenders with great records, but they're all down to earth. We have a nice family set-up — it's great. We all bounce off each other, and winning breeds winning.

"We have good friendships and we enjoy training. When you train with people you like and get on with, it makes the work pleasurable. Otherwise, boxing can be a fairly lonely, hard sport. It's one of the hardest games in the world. It's not very forgiving as it's just you fighting against the other guy; there's so much pressure when you're boxing because one off-day can ruin everything you've been working for."

His latest fight — a victory over hotly tipped American Jeff Lacy which saw the Welshman land more than 1,000 punches — was an example of the intensity at which he works.

He says, "It was unusual because it was a career-defining fight. I've been a champion for nine years but a lot of people will judge me on that fight because I was the underdog and people thought my opponent was going to walk all over me. The Americans were making him out to be the new mini-Tyson.

"There was so much pressure and, for me, the Lacy fight was like going for the world title for the first time again. I've never been so focused and motivated because I knew that failure would have meant me being known as a good world champion rather than a great one.

"I'd never trained so hard as I did preparing for that fight; I'd never been so psyched.

"Afterwards I had a good chill-out — the World Cup was on."

Relaxation is important and valued to this world champion.

He says, "I've got two boys, aged nine and 12. I like that they take up a lot of my time. Being a dad can be busy. I like to chill out — I'm a pretty chilled out guy. I like to go out sometimes and relax, socialise, but mainly I like watching films, going on holiday and eating, lots of eating!"

He's also aware that projects such as Terry Morris's Wales hall of fame illustrate how photography can be business and leisure.

He says, "I haven't got much knowledge of photography but my girlfriend's done a course in the subject, so maybe I'll have to take more notice. She's been talking to me about it quite a bit over the past few days — one of the things she'd like to do is wedding photography. Perhaps I'll ask Terry to give her a few tips."

Hall of Fame Fact File

- Joe Calzaghe was born in 1972.

- He began boxing as a primary school boy, growing up in Newbridge.

- Following a sparkling amateur career he made his professional debut in October 1993, at the old Cardiff Arms Park. On the night that Lennox Lewis beat Frank Bruno, Calzaghe beat Birmingham's Paul Hanlon.

- He beat Brighton's Chris Eubank for the WBO world super middleweight title in October 1997 and Florida's Jeff Lacy for the IBF version of the crown in March 2006.

Thanks

Terry Morris

To many who take an interest in my Cool Cymru project, it will seem like a solo undertaking — it's got my name on it, after all. However, this perception is wide of the mark. A team effort of the highest order, the process required a great deal of effort from others. They supplied encouragement, understanding, time, inspiration, expertise, knowledge, cheek, humour and joy. Those I thank include family, friends, colleagues, business partners and the celebrities who gave their own time to sit for me - for free.

In particular I thank my two sidekicks whose constant banter has ensured my feet have remained firmly on the ground.

I first got to know Andy Pearson as a workmate, but he has since become a good friend. A talented writer, he has used great skill to put into words the roller coaster ride of this project. He has given honest opinions and has helped me keep my focus. His dry wit and healthy cynicism has provided a constant reminder of who I am and what this project is all about. A cultural sponge with a wealth of knowledge, before each celebrity shoot he provided memorable briefs delivered in a range of dodgy accents. These will always stay with me.

Nothing has ever been too much trouble for my good friend Graham Harries. He was the documentary photographer for this project, and my lighting technician, Photoshop expert, props man, driver, comedian, tea maker and surrogate celebrity. His help, entertainment and advice proved invaluable.

My thanks also to all others who helped the collection succeed. They include those at Merlin Marketing and Public Relations, the Noah's Ark Appeal, Tinopolis (in particular, documentary producer Adam Salkeld), the Arts Council of Wales and Owens Road Services of Llanelli.

Thanks to Peter Gill and his talented colleagues at book publishers Graffeg and design consultancy Peter Gill & Associates.

Thanks to my buddy Jeff Connell, photographer extraordinaire, who taught me so much about photography and has always encouraged me to look at things from a different angle.

There are many others who have helped and supported me in many ways. They all know who they are. Many are mentioned in the book's main narrative.

Heartfelt thanks to my family: my mother and best friend Sheila has always supported me; my partner Laura has encouraged and believed in me from day one and has lived every high and low of this project with me; my children, Conor and Sadie May, brighten up every day and never let me forget what life is really about.

This book is dedicated to the memory of Cyril Williams, a grandfather and so much more.

Andy Pearson

Terry Morris followed a dream and made it come true. His Cool Cymru project, although not a matter of life and death, was a fine lesson in overcoming difficulty. It's not easy to convince managers and agents that their stars with busy lives should give valuable time — and little bits of their souls — for free. Everyone who helped make the project possible, especially Terry's great buddy Graham Harries, the people at Merlin Marketing and Public Relations and the stars themselves, are thanked for giving me the chance to take part in this adventure. Along the way I've often felt like a rather exposed tail gunner on a World War Two Lancaster raid, firing questions as Terry hit the target, but it's been wonderful fun. My friends at Swansea Council, my parents Jo and Terry and my in laws Alan and Margaret

are thanked for their backing. My biggest thanks go to my biggest pals — Claire, Ev and Mils. Incredibly, they seem to understand that good results can be achieved by the theft of time from family life. I love them, in part, for regularly allowing me to commit such a crime.

Graham Harries

When Terry asked me to help him out on the photo shoot with Charlotte Church little did I know what I was letting myself in for. It has been an exciting journey; a journey that has taken Terry's small, yet dedicated team to many places including the main Manchester United training complex, Chelsea Harbour ... and Hollywood! The spooky

thing is that last New Year's Eve I made a promise to myself to travel, and travel I have done thanks to Terry's vision. Cheers, mate. Our many hours of travelling have been made far easier by another star of the show, Andy Pearson. There's never a dull moment when you're around, pal. I owe big thanks to my best mate and partner, Jayne. You've never stopped me spending time on this project; time that I would have spent with you, love you. My parents are thanked for putting up with so much and getting me interested in photography. Sam, Beth, Meg, Kyle and Ross, cheers guys — you all make me smile so much.

Cool Cymru Collection

Cool